DYNAMICS

OF THE

WORD OF GOD!!

DYNAMICS

OF THE

WORD OF GOD!!

Dr Francis Madzivadondo

Chikavhu Publications

Contents

ACKNOWLEDGEMENTS		vii
chapter		ix

chapter		
1	Introduction	1
2	How do you make the blessing of God that is in you work?	6
3	Blessing and blessings?	11
4	Meditation of the word of God	17
5	You are responsible for your success in life	26
6	The Nature of God	30
7	The word of God sets you free	35
8	The word of God is wisdom.	39
9	Worry, Fear and Anxiety.	43
10	You are what God says you are	47
11	The Kingdom of God	54
12	The Word of God is Spirit and Life.	60
13	The Word of God is universal, permanent, and ignoring it brings judgement	66
14	The purposes of the word of God	69

15	Spirit of poverty.	77
16	The mindset of Jesus Christ.	81
17	Spiritual Authority	86
18	Belief	91
19	The Character of God	94
20	God cannot take you to your destiny without your involvement.	99
21	Principles	103
22	Revelation from the word of God brings a revolution in your life	107
23	Good heart?	112
24	Leadership In the Kingdom of God	118
25	Faith	122
26	Wealth	125
27	Conclusion	127

About The Author   129

ACKNOWLEDGEMENTS

Thanks for this book must be given and expressed to my dear wife Sandra my children Evans, his wife Amanda, Blessing, Nyasha and her husband Mustafa, Tinotenda, Tinashe, and grandchildren Munashe, Felisha, Tatenda, Prince and Caleb for the encouragement that they gave me and the support as I was writing this book. Professor Ezekiel and Dr Eunor Guti the apostles of Jesus Christ the founders of Forward In Faith Ministries International for mentoring me and moulding me into a minister of the Gospel of Jesus Christ that I am today. Thank you, my son, in law Mustafa Chikavhu for editing and doing all for this book to be a reality, you worked day and night for its success.

Joshua 1:8 "This book of the law shall not depart out of thy mouth; but thou shalt meditate therein day and night, that thou mayest observe to do according to all that is written therein: for then thou shalt make thy way prosperous, and then thou shalt have good success."

Copyright © 2022 by Dr Francis Madzivadondo

All rights reserved. No part of this book may be reproduced in any manner whatsoever without written permission except in the case of brief quotations embodied in critical articles and reviews.

First Printing, 2022

1

Introduction

Christianity is not about following certain rules and rituals, but it is your relationship with God. Jesus came to give life and change people so that people may live better lives, lived according to the plan and purpose of God. He came into the world to restore the plan of God about humanity which was destroyed by the devil in the garden of Eden. He came to bring back to man that which was stolen and destroyed by the devil. John 10:10 "The thief cometh not, but for to steal, and to kill, and to destroy: I am come that they might have life, and that they might have it more abundantly." All that we need in life has been packaged in us by God from the day we were created. Genesis 1:26 -28 [26] "And God said, let us make man in our image, after our likeness: and let them have dominion over the fish of the sea, and over the fowl of the air, and over the cattle, and over all the earth, and over every creeping thing that creepeth upon the earth.[27] So God created man in his own image, in the image of god created he him; male and female created he them.[28] And God blessed them, and said unto them , Be fruitful, and multiply, and replenish the earth, and subdue it: and have dominion over the fish of the sea, and over the fowl of the air, and over every living thing that moveth upon the earth"

Everything that we need physically and spiritually God has put it in us. We were not sent into the world empty. The physical things that we need were put in us in a spiritual form. The biggest problem that man has is that he does not know who he is in God and what is in him. After knowing who we are and what is in us then we must learn how to tap the treasure that is in us and make it work. People suffer because of lack of knowledge and demons are taking advantage of that. The word of God says God blessed man meaning that man was empowered to prosper and flourish in every area of his life. The hand of God, the favor of God, the authority of God was upon man in Eden before his fall, he was like God. God did not send man into the world empty, but he put everything that he needed into his spirit. Proverbs 4:23 "Keep thy heart with all diligence; for out of it are the issues of life." The heart which is referred in this instance is the spirit of a man. The life of man is in his spirit man, that is where he must operate from. People are suffering in the world because they are operating from the physical world. To be able to operate from the spirit man one must be born again and filled by the Holy Spirit.

In the garden of Eden, everything went wrong about man, the devil deceived him into disobedience and man lost everything that God had put in him. The blessing of God stopped working, it died within him. The condition for the life and blessing that was put in man by God is obedience. Genesis 3:17-19 [17] "And unto Adam he said, because thou hast hearkened unto the voice of thy wife, and hast eaten of the tree, of which I commanded thee, saying, Thou shalt not eat of it: cursed is the ground for thy sake; in sorrow shalt thou eat of it all the days of thy life; [18]Thorns also and thistles shall it bring forth to thee; and thou shalt eat the herb of the field;[19] In the sweat of thy face shalt thou eat bread, till thou return unto the ground; for out of it wast thou taken: for dust thou art, and unto dust shalt thou return." Everything about the plan of God upon man stopped working, died and man became a failure in every area of his life and every human being is born in this fallen state.

Although everything went haywire for man when he disobeyed God, God came with a plan to restore him back to his original position. 1 Corinthians 15: 21-22 [21] "For since by man came death, by man also came the resurrection of the dead. [22] For as in Adam all died, even so in Christ shall all be made alive." God had to bring his only begotten son into the world to restore the blessing in man that was stolen by the devil. John 3:16 "For God so loved the world, that he gave his only begotten son, that whosoever believe in him should not perish, but have everlasting life." When Jesus Christ comes into your life there are things that automatically change but some things you must do something for your life to change.

You must activate the blessing and the life of God that is dead in you that died in Eden. John 3:5 "Jesus answered, Verily, verily, I say unto thee, Except a man be born of water and of the Spirit, he cannot enter into the kingdom of God." For the life God and the blessing to come back to life first, you must be born again. To be born again is to have the life of Christ at work in you. The first sign that shows you that the life of Christ is at work in you is you start to hate sin and the fear of God comes upon you. You develop a passion for God and you start hating and stopping to do all the satanic things that you used enjoy doing. It is not just being a member of a church. To be born again is a spiritual thing that is real that produces results. It cannot be seen by the naked eye, but you and other people can start to see the changes in character that starts to happen.

After being born again you must be filled by the Holy Spirit. Acts

2: 1-4[1] "And when the day of Pentecost was fully come, they were all with one accord in one place. [2] And suddenly there came from heaven as of a rushing mighty wind, and it filled all the house where they were sitting. [3] And there appeared unto them cloven tongues like as of fire, and it sat upon each of them.[4] And they were all filled with the Holy Ghost, and begun to speak with other tongues, as the Spirit gave them utterance." Romans 8:14 "For as many as are led by the Spirit of God, they are the sons of God." If you are not born again you cannot have the Holy Spirit in you. Every change that will happen in your life by God through his word is based on you being born again and the Holy Spirit in you.

The word of God cannot work without the Holy Spirit. Ephesians 6:17 "And take the helmet of salvation, and the sword of the Spirit, which is the word of God." The word of God which must bring the life of God and the blessing of God to you cannot do so without the Holy Spirit, He makes the word of God to be alive. The word of God that is alive must deal with live satanic things that were deposited into our lives when Adam and Eve disobeyed God. Studying the word of God only without the Holy Spirit can only make you a legalistic person knowing what needs to be done but without the empowerment to do what must be done and the word cannot transform your life.

The Holy Spirit is the spirit of God that gives life and empowers the word of God to be effective. Hebrews 4:12 "For the word of God is quick, and powerful, and sharper than any two-edged sword, piercing even to the dividing asunder of soul and spirit, and of the joins and marrow, and is a discerner of the thoughts and intents of the heart."

After you are born again and filled by the Holy Spirit, and speaking in other tongues then you are ready to start the journey of transforming and changing your life by the word of God. You initiate every change that you want to happen in your life that is in accordance with the word of God. The Holy Spirit is our helper, he does not do things when we don't ask Him for help. We are given power when we become children of God so that we can change our lives John 1:12 "But as many as received him gave he power to become the sons of God, even to them that believe on his name."

Everything that you need in your life is in you, it has been brought back to life by the death and resurrection of Christ, but nothing works until you activate it by the word of God by the power of the Holy Spirit. You cannot enjoy the blessing of God until I do what you are supposed to do according to the word of God. You have a big part to play in changing your life and living the kingdom life that God has given you through Christ. Many times, children of God are waiting for God to change them. God has already done his part hundred percent through Jesus christ by bringing back the life and the blessing that had been stolen by the devil in Eden. Jesus Christ before giving up his ghost he shouted John 19: 30 "When Jesus therefore had received the vinegar, he said , It is finished: and he bowed his head, and gave up the ghost."

This means Jesus Christ finished the restoration work. It is now my work to appropriate that which Christ did on the cross. If I do nothing, I will also get nothing. This is why I say you have everything in you because if you have Jesus Christ living in you and him you then you have all the success and prosperity in every area of your life but you have to make it work as you are to discover as you continue studying this book. Joshua 1:8 "This book of the law shall not depart from your mouth, but you shall meditate on it day and night, so that you may be careful to do according to all that is written in it. For then you will make your way prosperous, and then will have good success.

2

How do you make the blessing of God that is in you work?

The blessing of God is within you it was put in you when God created you but unfortunately it was stolen and died when Adam disobeyed God. When you receive Jesus Christ when you get born again the blessing gets back to life the same way it was before the disobedience. The blessing is spiritual and empowers you to prosper and to flourish in every area of your life the same way that God flourishes because you are made in his image. This blessing gives you the nature of God. The blessing of God works only in the kingdom of God. Adam and Eve were in the kingdom of God and they had this blessing working in their lives but the moment they disobeyed God and were taken out of Eden it stopped working.

Therefore when you have Jesus you are in the kingdom of God. Luke 17:20 "And when he was demanded of the Pharisees when the kingdom of God should come, he answered them and said, The kingdom of God cometh not with observation: Neither shall they say, Lo here! Or, lo there! For, behold, the kingdom of God is within you." Everything that you need in life is in the kingdom of God therefore it follows that if you are in the kingdom of God you have access to that life.

You activate the blessing of God that is already in you through the word of God by the power of the Holy Spirit, holiness, righteousness, prayer, belief, and faith etc. You must develop kingdom life style for that blessing to work. You learn kingdom life style from the word of God. The blessing is not with someone or some were far it is within you. Many people are being deceived by their church leaders who claim to have the blessing of God. They ask money from people in exchange for it, all are lies of the devil. The following is how you activate the blessing. Joshua 1:8 "This book of the law shall not depart out of thy mouth; but thou shalt meditate therein day and night, that thou mayest observe to do according to all that is written therein: for then thou shalt make thy way prosperous, and then thou shalt have good success." The way to prosper in every domain of your life is by studying and meditating upon the word of God.

You must act upon that word that you are studying and meditating upon , the word must become your way of living and that is kingdom life style. If you just study and not live it then nothing is going to work. Everything that you believe in becomes part of your way of life. You are what you are because of what you believe, you are a product of your beliefs.

It is not God who shall make you prosper or succeed he has done his part which you could not do. Jesus did the impossible things that you could not do, and you must do what you can do by his word, God is not going to study for you. If you ignore studying his word, then stop thinking that anything is going to happen in your life from God. You could not take back the blessing and life that was stolen by the devil in the garden of Eden, it could only be done by Christ on the cross. Your life changes in relation to the knowledge that you have of the Lord Jesus Christ, the work that he did on the cross.

You cannot be ignorant of the ways of God and find yourself prospering according to the word of God. Hosea 4:6 "My people are destroyed for lack of knowledge: because thou hast rejected knowledge, I will also reject thee, that thou shalt be no priest to me: seeing thou hast forgotten the law of thy God, I will also forget thy children." 2 Peter 1:3 "According to his divine power hath given unto us all things that pertain unto life and godliness, through the knowledge of him that hath called us to glory and virtue." God is not going to do things in your life if you do not believe that he is able. You block yourself from getting what you are supposed to get from him because of lack of knowledge.

Ignorance of who God is is our greatest enemy not demons. God did not say my people are being destroyed by demons but he says by ignorance. Without the word of God and the power of the Holy Spirit at work in you, there is no change that you may witness in your life as a child of God. Isiah 55:10-11 [10]For as the rain cometh down, and the snow from heaven, and returneth not thither, but watereth the earth, and maketh it bring forth and bud, that it may give seed to the sower, and bread to the eater:[11] So shall my word be that goeth forth out of my mouth: it shall not return unto me void, but it shall accomplish that which I please, and it shall prosper in the thing whereto I sent it." You are like land, the land has all the potential to produce anything that you plant and if you plant nothing you get nothing out of it.

Everything that you need in life God has put it in your spirit man when he created you. Life is in your spirit, if you feed it with the word of God it will produce all the things that you need in life the physical things that you need. The word of God is the seed if it is planted in your spirit, it will germinate and give life to you. You have to impregnate your spirit man with the word of God and in turn you will give birth to success and prosperity in every area of your life.

The blessing that God put into you when you receive Jesus Christ is connected to the word of God. It cannot work although it is in you if you do not feed it with the word of God. Proverbs 4:20-23[20] "My son, attend to my words; incline thine ear unto my sayings. [21] Let them not depart from thine eyes; keep them in the midst of thine heart. [22] For they are life unto those that find them, and health to all their flesh. [23] Keep thy heart with all diligence; for out of it are the issues of life." Everything you need in life is hidden in the word of God and that word is within us, Christ is the word of God.

Deuteronomy 30:10-14 [10] "If thou shalt hearken unto the voice of the Lord thy God, to keep his commandments and his ststutes which are written in this book of the law, and it thou turn unto the Lord thy God with all thine heart,and with all thy soul. [11] For this commandment which I command thee this day, it is not hidden from thee, neither is it far off. [12] It is not in heaven, that thou shouldest say, who shall go up for us to heaven, and bring it unto us, that we may hear it, and do it? [13] Neither is it beyond the sea, that thou shouldest say, who shall go over the sea for us, and bring it unto us, that we may hear it, and do it?[14] But the word is very nigh unto thee, in thy mouth, and in thy heart, that thou mayest do it." The word of God is readily available to every- one. There is no reason for one not to use it. God is just he has made the word available for every human being.

It is very easy to believe in all other things but another to believe the word of God. The devil does not want you to believe the word of God because if you do he has got no power to stop you to become what the word says. Every human being is connected to God by his word and without his word, there is no connection. There are people who go to church, but they do not know the importance of the word of God and they do not have time to study it. If they are liked by the Pastor and are regularly prayed for by the Pastor, they think all is well with them. Your Pastor alone without the word of God cannot bring the change that God desires you to have. The blessing of God can only be activated by the word of God. Today people are being told to buy the so-called Holy Water and Holy Oil by their Pastors for them to have the blessing of God. All that is the lies of the devil, everything is in the word of God.

3

Blessing and blessings?

A blessing is a spiritual state that one gets into when one is born again when one becomes a child of God. The indwelling by the Lord Jesus Christ, the Holy Spirit and Father God in a person brings this spiritual state. This state empowers you to prosper and be successful in every domain of your life. John 14:20 "At that day ye shall know that I am in my Father, and ye in me, and I in you." The blessing empowers you to be able to do all things. Philippians 4:13 "I can do all things through Christ which strengthens me." The presents of God in your life makes you a blessed person. It is a spiritual mode that you get into when God takes residence in you. Without God, you cannot be blessed. Many people think that if a person has plenty of material things eg houses, cars, properties he is a blessed man.

That is not correct, anyone can have material things, those with God and those without. Material things are not the measurement of whether someone is blessed or not. Blessing as I explained earlier it is a spiritual state that only comes to a man because of having God. When Adam and Eve disobeyed God, they went into a cursed spiritual mode and all human beings are born in this spiritual mode. When Adam was put in the garden he had the blessing of God upon him, he was in a blessed spiritual mode. What it means is that the favour of God and the hand of God was upon him hundred per cent. This is what Jesus came to restore on the cross and everybody who believes in Jesus is automatically put back into the blessed spiritual mode.

The blessing of God comes in you automatically when we get born again but it does not operate in you automatically, it only operates when you fulfil certain conditions for example Joshua 1:8 "This book of the law shall not depart out of thy mouth; but thou shalt meditate therein day and night, that thou mayst observe to do according to all that is written therein: for then thou shalt make thy way prosperous, and then thou shalt have good success." You must study, meditate, and live the word. No human being can give you a blessing, it's only God who blesses you by his presence in you.

Blessing and blessings are two different things, but they are usually mixed up and confused many times. Blessings are good things that come to us because of the blessing of God that is in you, Without the blessing of God, you cannot get blessings from God. Many people when they talk about blessings, they just focus on material blessings, we get material blessings out of spiritual blessings which are superior to material ones. We should not focus on material blessings, they are added to you as rewards Matthew 6:33 "But seek ye first the kingdom of God, and his righteousness; and all these things shall be added unto you." Material blessings come to us because of spiritual blessings. Without the blessing of God, you cannot have the blessings of God.

The blessing of God transforms your life if you do what you are supposed to do according to the word of God. Our relationship with God is based on spiritual blessings and not on material blessings. Colossians3:1

-3 "If ye then be risen with Christ, seek those things which are above, where Christ sitteth on the right hand of God. [2] Set your affection on things above, not on things on the earth.[3] For ye are dead, and your life is hid with Christ in God." The devil is not ignorant of the word of God he knows it all that is why he works in collaboration with your flesh so that you may put your affection on things of this world. He does that to upset the working of the blessing of God that is in you. A spiritual blessing is what God says to you and what he says you can do through him by his word. Colossians 1:3 "Blessed be the God and Father of our Lord Jesus Christ, who hath blessed us with all spiritual blessings in heavenly places in Christ:" The spiritual blessings of God that we have been blessed with are spelt out in the word of God. We are going to have a look at very of them just to give examples.

You have been chosen to be a child of God.

Ephesians 1:4 "According as he hath chosen us in him before the foundation of the world, that we should be holy and without blame before him in love. We did not choose ourselves, but he chose us." Ephesians 1:5 -6 [5] "Having predestined us unto the adoption of children by Jesus Christ to himself, according to the good pleasure of his will, [6] To the praise of the glory of his grace, wherein he hath made us accepted in the beloved. The blessing of God is upon me because I have been accepted in the beloved son Jesus Christ." It is a spiritual blessing that you are a child of God, you have been favoured to be a child of God. It is the fundamental spiritual blessing to be a child of God. It is this blessing that comes with all the material blessings. The world is ignoring this and is running after material blessings which even if they get it they find no profit in it.

You have been chosen by God to be a chosen generation, a royal priesthood

1 Peter 2:9-10 [9] "But you are a chosen generation, a royal priesthood, an holy nation, a peculiar people; that ye should shew forth the praises of him who hath called you out of darkness into his marvellous light: [10] "Which in time past were not a people, but are now the people of God: which had not obtained mercy, but now have obtained mercy." It is the blessing of God that only could make you into this kind of a person nothing could have elevated you to that status ever. To be chosen to be among the chosen generation of God having God as your father is more than any material thing that you can ever have . Children of God ignore spiritual blessings as well and run after material blessings not knowing that the material is hidden in the spiritual blessing.

Redeemed through His blood.

Ephesians 1:6-8 [6] "To the praise of the glory of his grace, wherein he hath made us accepted in the beloved. [7] In whom we have redemption through his blood, the forgiveness of sins, according to the riches of his grace;[8] Wherein he hath abounded toward us in all wisdom and prudence." It is only by his blood that you were redeemed and that I was redeemed. Without redemption there is no way that you can enjoy the inheritance of the kingdom of God. You enjoy the blessings of God on condition that you have been redeemed. Redemption puts me into the blessed mode, or gives me the status of a blessed life.

You are now a partaker of the commonwealth of Israel.

Ephesians 2:6-22 [6] "And hath raised us up together, and made us sit together in heavenly places in Christ Jesus: [7] That in the ages to come he might shew the exceeding riches of his grace in his kindness toward us through Christ Jesus.[8] For by grace are ye saved through faith; and that not of yourselves: it is the gift of God: [9]Not of works, lest any man should boast.[10] For we are his workmanship, created in Christ Jesus unto good works, which God hath before ordained that we should walk in them.[11] Wherefore remember, that ye being in time past Gentiles in the flesh, who are called uncircumcision by that which is called the circumcision in the flesh made by hands; [12] That at that time ye were without Christ, being aliens from the commonwealth of Israel, and strangers from the covenants of promise, having no hope, and without God in the world:[13] But now in Christ Jesus ye who sometimes were far off are made nigh by the blood of Christ.[14] For he is our peace, who hath made both one, and hath broken down the middle wall of partition between us; [15] Having abolished in his flesh the enmity, even the law of commandments contained in ordinances; for to make in himself of twain one new man, so making peace;[16] And that he might reconcile both unto God in one body by the cross, having slain the enmity thereby:[17] And came and preached peace to you which were afar off, and to them that were nigh.[18]

For through him we both have access by one spirit unto the Father. [19]Now there- fore ye are no more strangers and foreigners , but fellowciticens with the saints, and of the household of God; [20] And are built upon the foundation of the apostles and prophets, jesus Christ himself being the chief cornerstone;[21] In whom all the building fitly framed together growth unto an holy temple in the Lord;[22] In whom ye also are builded together for an habitation of God through the spiri." The spiritual blessing of God always elevates you to greater heights, you have been raised from nothing to being seated together with the Father in heaven. You have been raised far above every principality and hence nothing can stop you from becoming what you must become according to the plan of God upon your life. You had no God but the blessing has made you a member of the household of God and a partaker of the commonwealth of Israel.

The inheritance given to us through Jesus Christ.

1 Corinthians 2:9-10 [9] "But as it is written, eye hath not seen, nor ear heard, neither have entered into the heart of man, the things which God hath prepared for them that love him. [10] But God hath revealed them unto us by his Spirit: for the Spirit searcheth all things, yea, the deep things of God." What you are in Christ and what he says you are is the blessing that brings blessings in your life." People are being deceived by some so-called men of God who claim that they carry the blessing and the blessings of God. The blessing and blessings of God are already in you they were packaged by God when he created you and were restored back to you by Jesus Christ on the cross after losing them to the devil when Adam and Eve disobeyed God. Spiritual blessings produce material blessings for example because of who you are in Christ all material things in this world are attracted to you, but these things do not just happen automatically you must believe the word of God and live it then you will start to have these things step by step. Your focus should not be on these material things but on Christ.

4

Meditation of the word of God

Meditation is done in many other disciplines that people practice, for example, Yoga, etc. In many other meditations that people do there are some spirits involved that are not of God but the meditation that I am taking about the meditation of the word of God involves the Holy Spirit. Without the Holy Spirit meditation of the word of God is impossible. The word of God is not active and cannot produce results if meditation is not done. The Webster dictionary says the following about meditation; "Penetrating or entering deeply into subjects of thought or thinking, having deep insight, or understanding. Penetrating to the depths of one's being."

Meditation is deep thinking that one does upon the word of God with the help of the Holy Spirit, and this is done prayerfully. This kind of thinking and prayer is done by a person in private and it can take many hours it is not rushed; it should go on in the spirit of the person even when he gets out of the prayer closet. The Holy Spirit must continue to teach you and minister to your spirit. Meditation allows your spirit to be connected to the spirit of God. During meditation, the Holy Spirit transfers the word of God that you have in your natural mind into your spiritual mind and the word is then processed in your spirit.

When you are meditating it is like you are in a classroom with the Holy Spirit teaching you things pertaining to the kingdom of God through his word. Meditation is fellowship with God through the Holy Spirit. The more time you spend fellowshipping with God the more you become like him and it brings a clear understanding of the word of God and you receive revelation. Revelation is when you see things spiritually and get supernatural understanding of the things of God that you cannot otherwise understand with your natural mind. When this happens you develop belief in God. Without revelation from the word of God you cannot believe in God and you cannot have faith in him. Meditation gives you the opportunity to dig deeper into the mysteries that are hidden in the word of God through the Holy Spirit. Read- ing the word of God only gives you raw information about God and that cannot help you to know God.

Meditation processes the word of God so that it becomes alive. Physically when you eat food that food has to be processed in your body before it gets into your blood system for it to nourish your body. It is the same spiritually, the word of God must be processed in your spirit so that it may affect the blessings of God that are in your spirit from the day you were created by God. Meditation makes the word of God that is in you to become useful and food to your spirit. If the word is in your mind only and not in your spirit it cannot be part of you and it cannot change your life.

The word of God must affect your thinking system even your anatomy and emotional system everything in your life and this only happens when you spend time meditating by the power of the Holy Spirit. Memorizing the word of God and speaking it in the flesh will never give you results. The word of God produces fruit only when you spend long periods of time meditating upon it. Meditation gives you spiritual understanding of the word of God.

When the word of God through meditation gets into your spirit these are some of the things that happen. God becomes so real to you the way your father, mother, friend are real in your life. When God shows you things in your spirit through the word of God those things become so real, and you have no doubt whatsoever and you start to tell people without even fear or doubt. You are convinced and confident and no man cannot stop you from doing what you are seeing in your spirit.

This is what happened to Abraham when God spoke to him what God said to him became so real that no man could stop him on embarking on the journey to the land that God had promised him. You see as if the thing has already happened although it is not yet manifested but to you it is as if it has already happened. This is faith as we see it from the word of God. Hebrews 11:1 "Now faith is the substance of things hoped for, the evidence of things not seen." Meditation produces faith and faith pleases God without faith we cannot get connected to God. Our dealings with God are all based upon faith. This is how faith is created by the word of God, it is not just by reading can you have faith, you must meditate upon the word. Romans 10:17 "Faith comes by hearing, and hearing by the word of God."

Do not keep the word of God in your natural mind, the mind is an enemy of the word of God. The mind does not accept the word of God, it is always against the word of God. 1 Corinthians 2:14 "But the natural man receiveth not the things of the spirit of God: for they are foolishness unto him: neither can he know them, because they are spiritually discerned ." Old wines skins in the bible stands for your natural mind and new wineskins stands for the spirit man. The old wine stands for all the human teachings that a person is taught. The new wine is the word of God. Matthew 9:16 -17 [16] "No man putteth a pice of new cloth unto an old garment, for that which is put in to fill it up taketh from the garment, and the rent is made worse.[17] Neither do men put new wine into old bottles: else the bottles break, and the wine runneth out, and the bottles perish: but they put new wine into new bottles, and both are preserved."

Your natural mind is not able to take the doctrine of Jesus Christ because it is full of the doctrine and the teachings of the devil and the world. Your spirit is the new wineskin and the word of God is the new wine, therefore, I say do not keep the word of God in your natural mind it does not work, the word of God only works when it gets into your spirit.

The word of God does not work anyhow, you need to understand how it works we need to be skillful. The word of God is spiritual therefore when you study it, you must do it spiritually. What do I mean by this? The word of God is spirit; John 6:63 "It is the spirit that quickeneth; the flesh profiteth nothing: the words that I speak unto you, they are spirit, and they are life." To be able to study the word spiritually it demands the Holy Spirit to be in you. He is the one who explains and teaches you the word that you are studying so that you get understanding. The Holy Spirit activates your spiritual man, and you start to understand the word of God by your spiritual mind not by your natural mind.

There is no change and transformation in your life, and you cannot live the word of God unless it has impacted your mindset, beliefs, character, and life, this happens during the time of meditation. Many people memorize scriptures and narrate them and you find there is nothing changing in their lives although they speak those scriptures, meditation is missing. Whatever you spend time meditating upon you will become that. If you are always meditating upon murder, you will become a murderer. If you spend time meditating on things that are contrary to the word of God, you open doors for demons to come and help you become what you are meditating upon. If you spend time meditating on the word of God, the Holy Spirit will come and help you become what you are thinking about.

Meditation transfers the word of God from your mind into your spirit. The word of God is food for the spirit man not for your mind. Your mind is only a passage that the word of God passes through, its destination is your spirit. David says, Psalm 119:11 "Thy word have I hid in mine heart, that I might not sin against thee." When the word is transferred into your spirit it now has the power to transform your life. When you speak it upon yourself or upon someone it has an effect because it is now alive. Hebrews 4:12 "For the word of God is quick , powerful, and sharper than any two- edged sword, piercing even to the dividing asunder of soul and spirit, and of the joints and marrow, and is a discerner of the thoughts and intents of the heart." Meditation gives you spiritual understanding of the word of God and revelation.

You are going to have new life as you meditate upon the word of God   2 Corinthians 5:17 "Therefore if any man be in Christ, he is a new creature: old things are passed away; behold, all things are become new. "Romans 6:4 "Therefore we are buried with him by baptism into death: that like as Christ was raised up from the dead by the glory of the Father, even so we also should walk in newness of life." The new life is the eternal life of God which is lived in the kingdom of God.

The new life is embedded in your spirit, Christ is that new life, which you get when receive him into your heart, however that life is not active until you start to study the word of God and to meditate upon it day and night. You do not just become new by just receiving Jesus Christ as your Lord and personal saviour. Being born again is just the initial stage and it is only done by God but the other stages he has left them to you to do. If you do not do what you are supposed to do you cannot enjoy the new life. God has given you tools that you must use so that you may be able to live this new life in the kingdom of God.

The tools are his word, the Holy Spirit, prayer , the blood of Jesus Christ the fivefold ministry according to Ephesians 4:11-12 [11] "And he gave some apostles; and some, prophets; and some, evangelists; and some, pastors and teachers; [12] For the perfecting of the saints, for the work of the ministry, for the edifying of the body of Christ:" There is no newness of life without the renewal of the mind first and foremost. Romans 12:2 "And be not conformed to this world: but be ye transformed by the renewing of your mind, that ye may prove what is that good, and acceptable, and perfect, will of God." Without you transforming your life by the word of God you cannot experience new life. God does not transform your mind it is your duty.

LET US SEE SOME STEPS TO RENEW YOUR MIND.

1. Feed the mind with the word of God
2. Meditate upon that word day and night,
   What you meditate upon that is what you become.
3. Practice, live what you meditate upon, that is what you will become.

You get your character from your mindset and your character points to your destiny. I can tell you what you shall become by simply watching what you do every day of your life unless you change. The word of God that you meditate upon must change the way you think, talk, and see things. The new life is in the word of God therefore you must spend time in it so that you may become what it is. You must become what the word of God says, it must manifest in you. You cannot operate in the kingdom of God with the same mind that you were born with, that mind is not compliant with the dynamics of the kingdom of God.

Everything about the new life starts from your spirit, it is born from your spirit. The word of God is the seed of your success. When the seed of the word of God gets into your spirit conception and germination take place. During meditation, the word fertilizes your spirit, and you conceive. It is like a woman when she has intercourse with a man when the seed of the man gets into her womb she conceives. Therefore, meditation upon the word of God brings to fruition the new life that is embedded in your spirit. Many wonder why they are not getting results in their lives; things are not changing ,it is because there is no word of God in them. Knowing the word only without meditation is like a woman who is barren even if she has sex with a man she cannot conceive. The seed is not meeting with the egg of a woman because she is barren.

The word of God must get into your spirit where there are eggs of prosperity and success. Success is in your spiritual DNA, the spirit of every human being has the DNA of God and God is success. Meditation is key when studying the word of God. The word of God is spirit, and you are spirit, the word must get into your spirit by the Holy Spirit for it to produce fruit. This transaction happens during meditation. When the word of God gets into your spirit it opens the eyes of your understanding and you get spiritual understanding, and you start to see in the spirit. Ephe- sians 1:18 "The eyes of your understanding being enlightened; that you may know what is the hope of his calling, and what the riches of the glory of his inheritance in the saints." When your spiritual eyes are opened you see the promises of God and they are so real as if the thing is already in the physical and yet it is not yet.

Matthew 13:3-9 [3] "And he spake many things unto them in parables, saying, behold, a sower went forth to sow; [4] "And when he sowed, some seeds fell by the wayside, and the fowls came and devoured them up: [5] Some fell upon stony places, where they had not much earth: and forthwith they sprung up, because they had no deepness of earth: [6]And when the sun was up, they were scorched; and because they had no root, they withered away. [7] And some among thorns; and the thorns sprung up, and choked them :[8] But other fell into good ground, and brought forth fruit, some an hundredfold, some sixtyfold, some thirtyfold.[9] Who hath ears to hear, let him hear." The word of God is the seed, and your spirit is the good ground.

Your mind is all the other grounds therefore do not keep the word in your mind it does not bear anything, it is enemy to the word of God. There are too many things going on in your mind that will destroy the seed which is the word of God. Your spirit is not against the word of God. Your spirit always says yes and amen to the word of God. When the word gets into your spirit its fruitful it will always bear fruit and it brings new life. It does the impossible, it brings healthy upon your body and you can overcome anything that comes your way. Psalm 119:97-100 [97]"O how love I thy law! It is my meditation all day. [98] Thou through thy commandments hast made me wiser than mine enemies: for they are ever with me.[99] I have more understanding than all my teachers: for thy testimonies are my meditation.[100] I understand more than the ancients, because I keep thy precepts. Psalm 49:3 "My mouth shall speak of wisdom; and the meditation of my heart shall be of understanding."

Isaiah 43:18 -19[18] "Remember ye not the former things, neither consider the things of old. [19]Behold, I will do a new thing; and now it shall spring forth; shall ye not know it? I will even make a way in the wilderness, rivers in the desert." Many Christians are bound by their past because there is no renewal of their mindset by the word of God. When you have a new mindset, when God brings a new thing you are ready to embrace it. You see yourself the way God sees you and you do not look at what is surrounding you and your ability, but you look at God and his ability.

You are failing in life because you are trying to live by the flesh, yet you are not flesh the essence of your being is spirit. Your flesh is fallen therefore there is nothing good that comes out of it except sin and failure. Romans 8:13 "For if ye live after the flesh, ye shall die: but if ye through the Spirit do mortify the deeds of the body, ye shall live." The word of God gives us spiritual and physical life and it sets us free from every bondage John 8:32 "And ye shall know the truth, and the truth shall make you free." Proverbs 3:1-8 [1] "My son, forget not my law; but let thine heart keep my commandments. [2] For length of days, and long life, and peace, shall they add to thee. [3] Let not mercy and truth forsake thee: bind them about thy neck; write them upon the table of thine heart: [4] So shalt thou find favour and good understanding in the sight of God and man. [5] Trust in the Lord with all thine heart; and lean not unto thine own understanding.[6] In all thy ways acknowledge him, and he shall direct thy paths.[7] Be not wise in thine own eyes: fear the LORD, and depart from evil. [8] It shall be health to thy naval and marrow to thy bones." All that people are looking for God has put it in his word and people are not aware of how they can get it.

I used to think that if I can memorise the word of God, I would get what it says but after many years I got discouraged because nothing was happening. I went before the Lord I wanted to understand why my life was stagnant. I fasted and prayed for many days until God started to teach me about meditation. I am writing this book to help someone who might be doing what I was doing just studying the word of God but doing nothing about meditation.

5

You are responsible for your success in life

Your relationship with God must prosper first if you are to succeed in every other area of your life. If your relationship is not growing, then you cannot have any other growth in your life. Matthew 6:33 "But seek ye first the kingdom of God, and his righteousness, and all these things shall be added unto you." The relationship cannot grow unless we fully get to know the one that we are in relationship with . We are only going to have a strong relationship if we engage ourselves fully with the word of God and the Holy Spirit to teach and to reveal to us the nature of God and his ways. Joshua was responsible for his success according to Joshua 1:8. He was promised success and prosperity by God if he followed the instruction that God gave him from his word. He wanted to go and conquer nations but he was not promised weapons of war by God, but he was told his success was in the word of God. He was told three things to do: -

1. The book of the law was not supposed to depart out of his mouth, he was to continuously speak the word of God and nothing of his
2. Was to meditate on the word of God day and night, which means all the time. He was not allowed to spend time thinking of fear or defeat or anything else that was outside the word of
3. He was to live according to the law that he was always speaking about and meditating

That was the package of his success and prosperity. If he did this everything else was going to fall in line on its own. Life is hidden in the word of God; it is not in those things that we are spending time doing. Your success is not in the weapons of war or any other tool but in the word of God. Your success is not with someone somewhere like I said earlier on in the book. It is buried in your spirit man according to Genesis 1:26-28 When God blessed man, he put everything that man needs in his spirit. When God assigned man to the world to dominate and to subdue it he did not send him empty. He gave him authority and all the resources that he needed, unfortunately man lost everything. God restored back those things back to man, the word of God is the key that unlocks the life of God that is in you.

Today we have some unscrupulous people who are deceiving people by claiming that they have some special powers to make people successful. There are too many false prophets who are going around asking people to give them money for them to be successful and prosperous in life, that is the lie of the devil. Everything you need is in you, and you are responsible for things that are happening in your life. If you are not successful it is your fault not God. Your success is in the word of God the same way it was with Joshua. The major purpose of Apostles, Prophets, Evangelists, Pastors, and Teachers in the body of Christ is to teach people the word of God so that people may know what is in them and what God has put in them, they cannot go further than that.

Ephesians 4:11-12 "And he gave some, apostles, and some prophets; and some, evangelists; and some, pastors and teachers; For the perfecting of the saints, for the work of the ministry, for the edifying of the body of Christ." These servants of God are not able to change your life, they cannot bring success and prosperity in your life they can only help you understand the word of God by teaching you.

You bring success in your life by the way you deal with the word of God that they teach you.

There is no way my relationship with God can prosper without the word of God. We see and learn the mind of God in his word, his ways, his character, promises, and his relationship with humanity. The formation of Christ in you which is done by the word of God causes the growth of my relationship with God. Galatians 4:19 "My little children, of whom I travail in birth again until Christ be formed in you." Strive always to live the word of God, if you do not live it nothing is going to change in your life. You must become the word, that happens as you study and meditate upon it. Many of us Christians are very good at saying scriptures, but we do not live them. As we do that, we are just wasting our time, demons know that God is, and they know all the scriptures but they do totally the opposite of what the word says. James 2:19-20 "Thou believest that there is one God; thou doest well; the devils also believe, and tremble. But wilt thou know, O vain man, that faith without works is dead?" If Joshua had ignored the word of God, he was going to fail in everything that he was doing. The same is for you if you ignore the word of God you will fail.

Success and prosperity do not come as an instantaneous miracle, it is progressive. It does not come while you are doing nothing, it is a decision that you must make, and you work towards it. Success and prosperity in the kingdom of God is not cheap as other people might think you must be ready to work very hard spiritually. You must dig deeper into the word of God, the deeper you go the more you understand the ways of God, it is in the ways of God that you encounter Success. Your positive response to the word of God will take you to your destiny, God has done all that he needed to do for you to be successful.

Your Pastor or your leader cannot take you to your destiny, this is a personal thing that you must do. Many times, I have seen Christians crying and asking God to make them successful. That is all wrong because God has already done everything when Jesus Christ died at Calvary, you must spend more time in the word of God to get knowledge and understanding instead of wasting time crying, do what you are supposed to do according to the word of God. The same instructions that were given to Joshua, what he was told to do with the word do the same and you will prosper. God does not do anything that is outside his word. Jeremiah 1:12 "Then said the Lord unto me, Thou hast well seen: for I will hasten my word to perform it." He is always watching over his word to do it, therefore if you want good results in your life live in the word of God. God is not moved by your emotions, but he is moved when you do things according to his word and when you do things by faith.

6

The Nature of God

The word of God is food to your spirit man, as you continue to feed upon it you will have the nature of Christ, and will start to live like him, think like him, and talk like him, all things will become possible and you will dominate every situation and subdue the earth. I want to help someone who is relying so much on his spiritual gift but has very little of the word of God. A spiritual gift does not make you spiritual person.. I am not saying all people who have spiritual gifts are not godly, but I am saying let us not be deceived by spiritual gifts. Godliness and spiritual gifts are two different things. You do not do anything to get a spiritual gift, it is given to you by God when you get born again and filled by the Holy Spirit. Spiritual gift does not make Godly, it is the word of God that does that. I have discovered that many people who are spiritually gifted have bad characters it is because they are not working on their lives through the word of God. They are just enjoying the fame that they have because of the spiritual gift that they have.

If you get a spiritual gift without wisdom that gift will destroy you and the people that follow you. You might be gifted but because you do not have the wisdom which you get from the word of God you end up destroying all the good work which you did by your spiritual gift. A spiritual gift does not build in you the nature of God, you develop the nature of God by his word. A spiritual gift does not make you a servant of God, but the word makes you into one. The spiritual gift does not give you the fear of God, but the word of God does. I have seen some preachers when they are on the pulpit preaching, they are wonderful but the moment they are off the pulpit they destroy the good work they were doing whilst on the podium by their old nature.

After receiving Christ, Christ must be formed in you by the word of God for you to be able to operate in the kingdom of God. When Christ is formed in you, get the ability to confront and deal with situations in the same manner that Christ did. Matthew 8:25-26 "And his disciples came to him, and awoke him, saying, Lord, save us: we perish. [26] And he saith unto them, Why are ye fearful, O ye of little faith? Then he arose, and rebuked the winds and the sea; and there was great calm. But the men marvelled, saying, What manner of man is this, that even the winds and the sea obey him!" Jesus Christ came to demonstrate the life of the Father through his life, and we are supposed to demonstrate the life of Jesus Christ through our lives. Galatians 2:20 "I am crucified with Christ: nevertheless I live; yet not I, but Christ liveth in me: and the life which I now live in the flesh I live by the faith of the son of God, who loved me, and gave himself for me."

When Christ is formed in us by the word of God, we get his mindset Philippians 2:5 "Let this mind be in you, which was also in Christ Jesus." Israel did not leave the slavery mindset of Egypt when they embarked on their journey into freedom. They left Egypt physically but they remained in Egypt in their minds. Numbers 11:4-6 [4] "And the mixt multitude that was among them fell a lusting: and the children of Israel also wept again, and said, Who shall give us flesh to eat? [5] We remember the fish, which we did eat in Egypt freely; the cucumbers, and the melons, and the leeks, and the onions, and garlic:[6] but now our soul is dried away: there is nothing at all, beside this manna, before our eyes." They could not embrace the freedom that God had given them because they continued with their slave mentality. There is no way one can have the nature of God without the mind of Christ.

When we have the nature of God all material things are attracted to us because all was created by him. Colossians 1:16 "For by him were all things created, that are in heaven, and that are in earth, visible and invisible, whether they be thrones, or dominions, or principalities, or powers: all things were created by him, and for him." Jacob wanted the blessing of God, yet he did not have the nature of God. God had to change him first, he had to give him his nature first before blessing him. By changing his name God was supernaturally giving him his nature. Genesis 32:28 "And he said, Thy name shall be called no more Jacob, but Israel: for as a prince hast thou fought with God and with men, and hast prevailed."

The name Jacob represented his old nature and Israel his new nature. When we have the nature of God every- thing is attracted to us even material things. Matthew 6:33 "But seek ye first the kingdom of God, and his righteousness; and all these things shall be added unto you." The blessing of Abraham does not work with the old nature it works with the new nature.

You become a partaker of the blessings of God through Christ therefore the more the nature of Christ is manifested the more the blessings are attracted to you. Ephesians 2:12-15 [12] "That at that time ye were without Christ, being aliens from the commonwealth of Israel, and strangers from the covenants of promise, having no hope, and without God in the world: [13] But now in Christ Jesus ye who sometimes were far off are made nigh by the blood of Christ.[14] For he is our peace, who hath made both one, and hath broken down the middle wall of partition between us; [15] Having abolished in his flesh the enmity, even the law of commandments contained in ordinances; for top make in himself of twain one new man ,so making peace." Therefore, the blessing of Abraham is attracted to the new nature. How you grow in God that is how you grow in the blessing of Abraham. The old nature is cursed, it is not compatible with the blessing of Abraham. The more godly you become the more you are moving nearer to the blessing of Abraham

When you have the new nature of God the following happens; you see the world with the eyes of God. You do not see things the way ordinary people do. You see yourself with the eyes of God, you start to understand your purpose why God created you, where you are coming from and where you are going.

Your priorities change, what you thought was very important in your life becomes the least you ever want to do. Philippians 3:8,10 -14 [8] Yea doubtless, and I count all things but loss for the excellency of the knowledge of Christ Jesus my Lord: for whom I have suffered the loss of all things, and do count them but dung, that I may win Christ, [10] That I may know him, and the power of his resurrection, and the fellowship of his sufferings, being made conformable unto his death;[11] If by any means I might attain unto the resurrection of the dead.[12] Not as though I had already attained, either were already perfect: but I follow after if that I may apprehend that for which also I am apprehended of Christ Jesus. [13] Brethren, I count not myself to have apprehended: but this one thing I do, forgetting those things which are behind, and reaching forth unto those things which are before, [14] I press toward the mark for the prize of the high calling of God in Christ Jesus." The new nature causes you to understand people more and why God loves them so much to the extent of laying down his life for them and it ushers you into the supernatural kingdom of God.You cannot enjoy the kingdom of God in your old nature, you need the new nature which you get as you progressively study, meditate and practice the word of God.

We are born into the supernatural kingdom of God by the word of

God and by his spirit. 1Peter: 1:23 "Being born of God, not of a corruptible seed, but of incorruptible, by the word of God, which liveth and abideth for ever." John 3:6 "That which is born of the flesh is flesh; and that which is born of the Spirit is spirit." The word of God gives us the supernatural nature of God. Mark 16:17 -18 [17] "And these signs shall follow them that believe; In my name shall they cast out devils; they shall speak with new tongues; [18] They shall take up serpents; and if they drink any deadly thing, it shall not hurt them; they shall lay hands on the sick, and they shall recover." The changes that are now in your life are made possible by the supernatural nature of God that is brought by the word of God through the power of the Holy Spirit. You activate the nature of God that is in us which we got when we got born again by the word of God, without the word of God that nature stops working and we become ordinary as everyone else in the world.

7

The word of God sets you free

John 8:31-32 [31] "Then said Jesus to those Jews which believed on him, If ye continue in my word, then are ye my disciples indeed. [32] And ye shall know the truth, and the truth shall make you free. The word of God protects us from getting lost. 1 Timothy 4:1 "Now the spirit speaketh expressly, that in the latter times some shall depart from the faith, giving heed to seducing spirits, and doctrines of devils." Religion is doing everything else with so much commitment, even sacrificially but without the spiritual knowledge of the word of God. One may become very zealous but without knowledge. Romans 10:1-3 [1] "Brethren, my heart's desire and prayer to God for Israel, is that they might be saved. [2] For I bear them record that they have a zeal of God, but not according to knowledge. [3] For they being ignorant of God's righteousness, have not submitted themselves unto the righteousness of God."

The word of God activates the nature of God that is in us and sets us free from strongholds of the devil that are in our minds. Ephesians 4:21-25 [21] "If so be ye have heard him, and have been taught by him, as the truth is in Jesus: [22] That ye put off concerning the former conversation the old man, which is corrupt according to the deceitful lusts; [23] And be renewed in the spirit of your mind; [24] And that ye put on the new man, which after God is created in righteousness and true holiness. [25] Wherefore putting away lying, speak every man truth with his neighbour: for we are members one of another." The word of God pulls down every stronghold that is in your life. 2 Corinthians 10:4-5 [4] "(For the weapons of our warfare are not carnal, but mighty through God to the pulling down of strongholds;) [5] Casting down imaginations, and every high thing that exalteth itself against the knowledge of God, and bringing into captivity every thought to the obedience of Christ;" Everybody has some strongholds that you must fight with in life.

A stronghold is a belief that you base your life upon, but it is contrary to the truth of the word of God. The world is being run by the devil and he is a liar, it then follows that the lives of the people are being lived based on the lies of the devil. What you think is normal on this planet earth is abnormal, the world has accepted this abnormality as our normal. These strongholds the lies of the devil cause us to doubt the word of God. It is only the word of God through the power of the Holy Spirit that can destroy these strongholds. Jeremiah 23:29 "Is not my word like as a fire? Saith the lord; and like a hammer that breaketh the rock in peaces." We must be set free by the word of God; this is the freedom that we need more than the political freedom etc. Political freedom can never change our lives, but freedom of the mind totally liberates us. Paul could encourage people who were not in jail and yet he was in jail, the jail could not take away his liberty and joy because he was free in his mind. Philippians 4:4 "Rejoice in the LORD always: and again I say Rejoice."

|The word of God is food for the spirit man it is not a weapon to use to do biblical or theological arguments. 2 Timothy 2:14-16 [14] "Of these things put them in remembrance, charging them before the Lord that

they strive not about words to no profit, but to the subverting of the hearers. [15] Study to shew thyself approved unto God, a workman that needeth not to be ashamed, rightly dividing the word of truth. [16]But shun profane and vain babblings: for they will increase unto more ungodliness." Matthew 4:4 "But he answered and said, It is written, Man shall not live by bread alone, but by every word that proceedeth out of the mouth of God." Some have been made to believe that the word of God works like magic to acquire material things they have been told that whatever they want they must just speak the word and they will get it.

The word of God is not cheap it is God himself, without a relationship with him it does not work, outside of Him it does not work. The word that has power to change your life and sets you free is the word of God that you speak from your spirit. Many people try to declare things with the word from their mouth and mind it does not work, power is in the Holy Spirit mixed with the word that you have hid in your spirit. Speak the word of God by your spirit man, speak from your spirit not just from your natural mind. Job 22:28 "Thou shalt decree a thing, and it shall be established unto thee: and the light shall shine upon thy ways."

The devil binds people by his word through the power of his spirit and nothing can undo this bondage in this world except the word of God through the power of the Holy Spirit. Words are so powerful therefore you must not just speak anyhow upon your- self or your children because what you say will always come to pass. The words that you speak if they are ungodly the devil will enhance those words by his spirit. If they are godly the Holy spirit will enhance them, and they become reality. It may take time but eventually what you have said will always come to pass unless they are reversed.

In the world of witchcraft, they understand the power of words. When they bewitch someone, they do it by speaking what they want to happen to their victim, as they speak those words, they will be under the power of demons which enhances and make sure they go and do exactly what was spoken upon the victim. Demons are servants of those people who practice witchcraft. This is what the children of God must do as well. We must speak the word of God upon our lives that which we want to happen in our lives according to the will of God. When you speak you must be under the power of the Holy Spirit who enhances and does exactly what the word of God says. Many of us Christians are just waiting for God to do things for us.

We set ourselves free from the curses of the devil by speaking the word of God in every situation that we find ourselves in. When you find yourself in a situation do not run to get prayed for by the Pastor etc. speak to the situation yourself, if you are a child of God, you have power in you therefore, every child of God must be filled by the Holy Spirit, without the Holy Spirit even if you speak the word of God there is nothing that is going to happen. When you speak as a child of God the Holy Spirit will go and do what you have instructed him to go and do by the word of God. The Holy Spirit has been given by God to do what we instruct him to do by the word of God. He only does things that you instruct him to do through the word of God, out of the word of God he does nothing.

8

The word of God is wisdom.

To live successfully and fully in this world we need the wisdom of God that we only get from the word of God. There is human wisdom and the wisdom of the world. I am talking about the wisdom of God which is supreme. Proverbs 4:7 "Wisdom is the principal thing ; therefore get wisdom: and with all thy getting get understanding." The wisdom of God is nothing more than his word, his ways, his thoughts, and doings. Every move of God is wisdom and that is the way that children of God must live. Proverbs 9:10 "The fear of the Lord is the beginning of wisdom: and the knowledge of the holy is understanding." The fear refers to reverencing what God says, if you reverence what God says and do it you are considered a wise man. You cannot reverence instructions that are given by someone whom you do not trust and have confidence in. Ephesians 1:17-18 [17]That the God of our Lord Jesus Christ, the Father of glory may give unto you the spirit of wisdom and revelation in the knowledge of him:[18] The eyes of your understanding being enlightened; that ye may know what is the hope of his calling, and what the riches of the glory of his inheritance in the saints," People are suffering in life because they have chosen to live by their own wisdom the wisdom of the world and hence wrong decisions are made which put them in trouble.

Studying scriptures only cannot bring a relationship between you and God, you need the spirit of wisdom and revelation who is the Holy Spirit to be in you. John 5:39 "Search the scriptures; for in them ye think ye have eternal life: and they are they which testify of me." You need to be introduced to the one who is being spoken of by the scriptures first, there must be a relationship, a connection first. Your brain and mind cannot comprehend the things of God. 1 Corinthians 12:14 "Now we have received, not the spirit of the world, but the spirit which is of God; that we might know the things that are freely given to us of God. Which things also we speak, not in the words which man's wisdom teacheth, but which the Holy Ghost teacheth; comparing spiritual things with spiritual. But the natural man receiveth not the things of the Spirit of God: for they are foolishness unto him: neither can he know them, because they spiritually discerned."

We become wise by living like Jesus Christ he is the wisdom of God and the word of God. Christ came to demonstrate the life of the Father therefore wisdom is living like Christ. The characteristics of Christ is wisdom, Christ lived the word of God, he walked the talk. Many Christians are not wise because they do not live the scriptures, they can only narrate them but live something else.

Wisdom brings a genuine love of God and wise people can forgive those who trespass against them. Wisdom is patient and is passionate for people John 3:16 "For God so loved the world, that he gave his only begotten Son, that whosoever believeth in him should not perish, but have everlasting life." Galatians 5:22-23 But the fruit of the Spirit is love, joy, peace, longsuffering, gentleness, goodness, faith, meekness, temperance, against such there is no law." Wise people have the righteousness of God. 2 Corinthians 5:21 "For he hath made him to be sin for us, who knew no sin; that we might be made the righteousness of God in him." Wise people seek peace always with all men. Hebrews 12:14 "Follow peace with all men, and holiness, without which no man see the Lord." Wise people grow in favor with both man and God. Luke 2:52 "And Jesus Christ increased in wisdom and stature, and in favor with both man and God."

Wise men live for God, they do to others what they want done to them. Luke 6:31-35 [31] And as ye would that men do to you, do ye also to them likewise. [32] For if ye love them which love you, what thank have ye? For sinners also love those that love them.[33] And if ye do good to them which do good to you, what thank have ye? For sinners also do even the same. [34] And if ye lend to them of whom ye hope to receive, what thank have ye? For sinners also lend to sinners, to receive as much again. [35] But love ye your enemies, and do good, and lend, hoping for nothing again; and your reward shall be great, and ye shall be the children of the Highest: for he is kind unto the unthankful and to the evil." This is what happens when you have the wisdom of God, and you can learn that as a child of God you still have a lot to do for you to consider yourself as having the wisdom of God. Wise men walk by faith and not by sight and live to do the will of God. 2 Corinthians 5:7 "For we walk by faith, not by sight." John 6:8 "For I came down from heaven, not to do mine will, but the will of him that sent me."

A man may have all the wisdom of the world but if he does not have the wisdom from the word of God, he is considered a fool. 1 Corinthians 1:19 "For it is written, I will destroy the wisdom of the wise, and will bring to nothing the understanding of the prudent." 1 Corinthians 1:25 "Because the foolishness of God is wiser than men, and the weakness of God is stronger than men."

The inheritance of the kingdom of God is for the wise not for fools. Many want the inheritance of the kingdom of God, but they are doing nothing to acquire the wisdom of God. Proverbs 3:35 "The wise shall inherit glory: but shame shall be the promotion of fools." A fool according to the word of God is someone who does not have God and someone who is ignorant of the word of God. Even if you go to church and claim to be born again but if you are ignorant of his word you are a fool. The blessing of Abraham is for the wise, wise people live in obedience to God like Abraham. Genesis 12 :1-4 [1] "Now the Lord had said unto Abram thee out thy country, and from thy kindred, and from thy father's house, unto a land that I will shew thee. [2] And I will make of thee a great nation, and I will bless thee, and make thy name great; and thou shalt be a blessing:[3] And I will bless them that bless thee, and I curse him that curseth thee: and in thee shall all families of the earth be blessed.[4] So Abram departed, as the Lord had spoken unto him; and Lot went with him: and Abram was seventy and five years when he departed out of Haran." The prerequisite for you to enjoy the blessing of Abraham is wisdom don't just pray to get it pray for wisdom as well.

Many Christians want the blessings of God but they are not aware that the things of God are enjoyed by those who have the wisdom of God. God does not bless fools. The prerequisite for the blessings of God is wisdom. Wealth is not given to fools in the kingdom of God.Fools are destroyed by their prosperity. Proverbs 1:32 "For the turning away of the simple shall slay them, and the prosperity of fools shall destroy them." You must first have the wisdom of God to be able to handle prosperity and success before God grants it to you.God does not just grant you success yet you are a fool because he does not want your distruction. It is only the devil who gives prosperity to fools to destroy them. Develop to be wise to enjoy the prosperity and the success from God.

9

Worry, Fear and Anxiety.

10 Crucial Differences Between Worry and Anxiety by Guy Winch Ph.d. Psychology Today . "We tend to experience worry in our heads and anxiety in our bodies. Worry tends to be specific while anxiety is more diffuse. Worry is verbally focused while anxiety includes verbal thoughts and mental imagery. Worry often triggers problem solving but anxiety does not. Worry creates mild emotional distress, anxiety can create severe emotional distress. Worry is caused by more realistic concerns than anxiety. Worry tends to be controllable, anxiety much less. Worry tends to be a temporary state but anxiety can linger." When God created man, he wired him in such a way that he cannot live successfully without being connected and dependent on him.

When man disconnects himself from God he is attacked by fear, worry, and anxiety when he is confronted by challenging circumstances. The word of God drives away fear, worry, and anxiety because it gives hope and courage. Having knowledge of the word of God gives one confidence and knowledge that God is on your side even if you are going through issues, it drives away all the fear out of you. Isaiah 43:2 "When thou passest through the waters, I will be with thee; and through the rivers, they shall not overflow thee: when thou walkest through the fire, thou shalt not be burned; neither shall the flame kindle upon thee." Psalm 23: 4 "Yea, though I walk through the valley of the shadow of death, I will fear no evil: for thou art with me; thy rod and thy staff they comfort me."

The word of God says man cannot live by bread alone but by every word that comes out of the mouth of God, but people have nothing to do with the word of God that is why the world is full of fear, worry, and anxiety. People go to doctors to seek treatment when they suffer from anxiety, there is no treatment for such things medications that are given can only suppress what is happening but they cannot heal.

The treatment is the word of God not medication from doctors. Fear, worry, and anxiety are spiritual problems that attack people who do not have the word of God. If you do not want to suffer from these emotional problems study the word of God and put your confidence in God and the problems will disappear. Some people are taking alcohol and abusing drugs because they are trying to run away from fear and worry. Unfortunately, this is temporary when they get sober the situation is still staring at them even harder.

If only you understood how important the word of God is in your life, you would invest more time studying it and meditating upon it day and night. Psalm 1:1-3 [1] "Blessed is the man that walketh not in the counsel of the ungodly, nor standeth in the way of sinners, nor sitteth in the seat of the scornful. [2] But his delight is in the law of the Lord, and in his law doth he meditate day and night. [3] And he shall be like a tree planted by the rivers of water, that bringeth forth his fruit in his season; his leaf also shall not wither; and whasoever he doeth shall prosper." People fail in doing so many things because they do it without God.

Worry is destroying many people because they have faith in themselves, they ignore the word of God and do things their own way.

Philippians 3:4-8 [4] "Though I might also have confidence in the flesh. If any other man thinketh that he hath whereof he might trust in the flesh, I more: [5] Circumcised the eighth day, of the stock of Israel, of the tribe of Benjamin, a Hebrew of the Hebrews; as touching the law, a Pharisee; [6] Concerning zeal, persecuting the church; touching the righteousness which is in the law, blameless.[7] But what things were gain to me, those I counted loss for Christ. [8] Yea doubtless, and I count all things but loss for the excellency of the knowledge of Christ Jesus my Lord: for whom I have suffered the loss of all things, and do count them but dung, that I may win Christ." If you rely on God and not on yourself you will never suffer from fear of the unknown, anxiety and depression.

Babies do not suffer from these conditions because they have no confidence in themselves everything is upon the shoulders of their parents. Put everything into the hands of your father God and you shall be free and enjoy life. Putting things in the hands of God is not as simple as all that, you must learn how to do it. You cannot put your trust in God if you do not understand him, and that under-standing you get it from the word of God by the power of the Holy Spirit. You can only be immune to the attacks of the devil through your mind if you renew your mind with the word of God.

Worry is a result of meditating on negative things happening in our lives or that happened some other time, we worry, and the worry develops into anxiety. All this can be stopped by the word of God, it is medicine for your body, soul, and spirit. If you do not have it, you will have problems with your body, your emotions, and your spirit. Colossians 3:16 "Let the word of Christ dwell in you richly in all wisdom; teaching and admonishing one another in psalms and hymns and spiritual songs, singing with grace in your hearts to the Lord." Worry comes because you are full of the words of the devil, you meditate upon those words day and night and the result is fear, de-pression, and anxiety. Worry does not change your situation, but the word of God has the power to change situations Fear incapacitates you and paralyzes you but the word of God empowers you to conquer and overcome every situation.

The word of God is medicine, food , wisdom, it all that we need in life but it has been hidden to you by the devil. The word of God does not have side effects like all the medicines that people take. , it is pure.

10

You are what God says you are

When you are born into this world biologically, you do not understand who you are and why you have been born, or the purpose of your living. You start to slowly understand these dynamics when you get born again when Christ comes into your life as Lord and Saviour. As you study the word of God through the power of the Holy Spirit, you start to understand who you are and where you came from, where you are going and your purpose on earth. No man knows you better than God, therefore do not listen to what they say that you are.

Your story is all embedded in the word of God and is with him. If you want to understand more about yourself, go to him and ask him. Judges 6:12-17 [12] "And the angel of the Lord appeared unto him, and said unto him, The Lord is with thee, thou mighty man of valour. [13] And Gideon said unto him, Oh my Lord, if the Lord be with us, why then is all this befallen us? and where be all his miracles which our fathers told us of, saying, Did not the Lord bring us up from Egypt? But now the Lord hath forsaken us, and delivered us into the hands of the Midianites. [14] And the Lord looked upon him, and said, Go in this thy might, and thou shalt save Israel from the hand of the Midianites: have not I sent thee? [15]And he said unto him, Oh my Lord, wherewith shall I save Israel? Behold, my family is poor in Manasseh, and I am the least in my father's house. [16] And the Lord said unto him, Surely I will be with thee, and thou shalt smite the Midianites as one man. [17] And he said unto him, If I have found favour grace in thy sight, then shew me a sign that thou talkest with me." God was seeing a mighty man of valour in Gedeon, but he did not know who he was and what he could accomplish through God.

He saw himself as a very useless person because of his background. You cannot know who you are if you spend most of your time with people and examining the bad things that happened to you in your past.

You will become what they think you are or what you think you are. Jesus Christ came to make you into another new man with new abilities that you never thought you could ever have. Spend time in the word of God, you will discover who you are and what you can achieve with God. The world is under a spiritual slumber which can only be taken away by the word of God. I was in that slumber, but I thank God for awakening me through his word and his Spirit. If you spend more time in the spirit in which you are ushered in by the word of God, you will shine in this world of the living.

Daniel understood by books, by the word of God he became a genius in the affairs of the world during his time. He excelled in everything that he did and was a wise man because of the word of God that was in Him. The word of God develops you into a spiritual person and when you are spiritual you will be able to live better in this world. The world that you are living in is physical, but it is spiritual at the same time because it was made from the spirit and is run by spiritual laws.

These spiritual laws are all spelt out in the word of God. Daniel 9:2 "In the first year of his reign I Daniel understood by books the number of the years, whereof the word of the Lord came to Jeremiah the prophet, that he would accomplish seventy years in the desolations of Jerusalem." Shadreck, Misheck and Abednego were spiritual they saw and knew what the majority could not see, the rest had no understanding of what they were worshipping. The three had sound knowledge of the word of God that is why even the king could not move them to worship the idol. Daniel 3:16-18 [16] "Shadreck, Meshach, and Abednego, answered and said to the king ,O Nebuchadnezzar, we are not careful to answer thee in this matter. [17]If it be so, our God whom we serve is able to deliver us from the burning fiery furnace, and he will deliver us out of thine hand, O king. [18] But if not, be it known unto thee, O king, that we will not serve thy gods, nor worship the golden image which thou hast set up." When you have the knowledge of the word of God you cannot be influenced or forced to worship something else that is not God. I concur with people who say that knowledge is power.

The three young men did not have any weapons of war to fight with against the king and all the people that were against them. Their only weapon, was the knowledge of the word of God and they prevailed. Acts 19:20 "So mightily grew the word of God and prevailed." With the word of God, you are able to prevail in life it does not matter what you are facing. There is no power that surpasses the power that is in the word of God in this world.

The truth about you and all that is happening in the world is in the word of God. Facts are not the truth, truth is more than facts. It is a fact that you can get sick, but the truth is that you are not supposed to be sick because Christ took your sickness upon himself. Facts are things that people see on the ground and they believe in those things, but the truth is what God says. The truth is God himself who does not change, and he is the word of God. John 1 :1,14 [1] "In the beginning was the Word, and the Word was with God, and the Word was God. [14] And the Word was made flesh, and dwelt among us, (and we beheld his glory, the glory as of the begotten of the Father,) full of grace and truth." The world has been misled by facts; facts are not the truth.

We must not live by facts, but we must live by the truth of God which is the word of God. No man has the truth therefore you are not what the world is saying. You are what God says you are, you have all that God says you have. You must believe in the word of God to be what God says you are. The world has been told that it came into being as a result of a big bang and they are believing it, It is even being taught in schools. They have also been told that humans evolved from a chimpanzee and it has been accepted because they do not know the truth. If people evolved from a chimpanzee why are we not seeing them today in the process of developing, what has stopped the evolution? Lies of the devil.

There is no other book in this world except the bible that can tell us about the origin of man and where he is going after his time on earth. It is the only book that explains the dealings of the creator and the creature. According to God, you can do all things through him, you are a success and not a failure. God has made you into a king and a priest. Revelation 1:5-6 [5] "And Jesus Christ, who is the faithful witness, and the first begotten of the dead, and the prince of the kings of the earth. Unto him that loved us and washed us from our sins in his own blood, [6] "And hath made us kings and priests unto God his Father; to be glory and dominion forever and ever. Amen." When God looks at you, he is seeing a king but people do not see you that way because they do not know you.

I will try to make you see who God says you are in some examples from the word of God. You have been crowned with honour and glory because of Jesus Christ. Whatever has happened to Christ after his death and resurrection that is who you are. Hebrews 2:9 "But we see Jesus who was made a little lower than the angels for the suffering of death, crowned with glory and honour; that he by the grace of God should taste death for every man." As he was crowned with glory you are also crowned with that same glory because you are in him.

People see you as a useless person but in Christ you are glorified. You have inherited all that Jesus Christ inherited from the Father. When God looks at you, he sees you as an heir but you see yourself the way Gedeon saw himself. Ephesians 1:1 "In whom also we have obtained an inheritance, being predestined according to the purpose of him who worketh all things after the counsel of his own will." Romans 8:17 "And if children, then heirs of God, and joint -heirs with Christ; If be that we suffer with him, that we may be also glorified together." This is again who you are, seated together with Christ at the right hand of God in heaven. Mark 16:19 "So then after the Lord had spoken unto them, he was received up into heaven, and sat on the right hand of God." As all this was happening you were in him and that is where you are right now at the right hand of the Father.

You are not ordinary; you are supernatural, you are here on earth and at the same time seated in heaven. You are extraordinary if you continue to feed on the word of God doing extraordinary things is your portion. People judge you by what they see outwardly but they are ignorant of what God has put in you through Christ. The problem goes further even yourself you are not aware of what God has put into you. You only know that you are a child of God, and it ends there. The biggest task that you have is to discover who you are in Christ, and you can only do this by investing many hours searching scriptures with the help of the Holy Spirit.

You are rich and you are not poor. People associate being rich with having material things. That is what the world believes in but that is not correct. A person can have all the material things in the world yet being the poorest person, and vice versa a person may not have any material thing, yet he is the richest. Christ had no material thing at all even a place to put his head to sleep yet he was the richest man who ever lived on earth.

It is a big curse for a man to be rich with material things but without God. Mark 8:36 "For what shall it profit a man, if he shall gain the whole world, and lose his own soul." Some children of God cannot testify that they are rich because they think being rich is when they have material things, they are not aware that they are already rich because of Jesus who is in their lives. God says to you, that you cannot fail if you are in Christ. You used to be a failure but not now with the nature of Christ in you, you are a success in all situations. Philippians 4:13 "I can do all things through Christ which strengthened me." Through Christ you now have extraordinary capacities that Christ has, you must not look down upon yourself. You are an overcomer through Christ who has overcome the world. John 16:33 "These things I have spoken unto you, that in me ye might have peace. In the world ye shall have tribulation: but be of good cheer;

I have overcome the world." Knowing what God says about you and who you are in him will transform your life in a mighty way. If you continue to see yourself as the same man that you were before Christ came into your life is disastrous because there is no way you can change if your way of seeing things is the same. You are now a new creature or creation because of Christ. You are now born of God and not of man. 2 Corinthians 5:17 "Therefore if any man be in Christ, he is a new creature: old things are passed away; behold, all things are become new." Everything about you has become new because of Christ.

Many Christians get confused also with this verse. When Paul was writing this statement, he was seeing a finished product. You do not become a new creation overnight, but you become one step by step as you obey the instructions of God through his word and Spirit. The old things stand for your old nature, which was cursed, sick, and poor. The new nature has been raised together with Christ as a superman followed by the blessings grace and the favour of God. You are now born of the incorruptible seed of the word of God. Galatians 2:20 "I am crucified with Christ: nevertheless I live; yet not I, but Christ liveth in me: and the life which I now live in the flesh I live by the faith of the son of God, who loved me, and gave himself for me." Your life is now in the new man, success and prosperity are in this new man, all the promises of God have been made to the new man not to the old man.

You are now a member of the household of God, you are no longer a foreigner or an alien to the commonwealth of Israel because of Jesus Christ. This gets me to be excited and this chapter of the bible has really changed my life, there is now nothing that can stop me in any way. Ephesians 2: 13 -19 [13] "But now in Christ Jesus ye who sometimes were far off are made nigh by the blood of Christ. [14] For he is our peace, who hath made both one, and hath broken down the middle wall of partition between us; [15] Having abolished in his flesh the enmity, even the law of commandments contained in ordinances; for to make in himself of twain one new man, so making peace;[16] And that he might reconcile both unto God in one body by the cross, having slain the enmity thereby: [17] And came and preached peace to you which were afar off, and to them that were nigh, [18] For through him we both have access by one Spirit unto the Father.

Now therefore ye are no more strangers and foreigners, but fellow citizens with the saints, and of the household of God." I have given you some examples of what God sees when he looks at you, he sees himself in you, therefore, see yourself the same way when you look at yourself. Gedeon saw a useless man when he looked at himself but God was seeing a mighty man of valour.

11

The Kingdom of God

It is a spiritual kingdom, and we are born into it by the word of God and the Holy Spirit. John 3:3-6 [3] "Jesus answered and said unto him, Verily, Verily, I say unto thee, Except a man be born again, he cannot see the kingdom of God.[4] Nicodemus saith unto him, How can a man be born when he is old? Can he enter the second time into his mother's womb? [5] Jesus answered, Verily, Verily, I say unto thee, Except a man be born of water and the Spirit, he cannot enter into the kingdom of God. [6] That which is born of the flesh is flesh; and that which is born of the Spirit is Spirit."

The kingdom of God operates upon the principles of the word of God. Without a sound spiritual understanding of the word of God, we cannot operate in it. We walk in the king- dom by faith, by what the word of God says. 2 Corinthians 5:7 (For we walk by faith, not by sight.) When we understand the kingdom of God by scriptures and the Spirit of God all things become possible to you. Matthew 19:26 "But Jesus beheld them, and said unto them, With men that is impossible; but with God all things are possible." The kingdom of God is supernatural, it works with the word of God that is supernatural, everything else shall come to an end but the word of God abides for ever. You are body, soul and spirit, your flesh and blood are corrupt they cannot operate in this kingdom. 1Corithians 15:50 "Now this I say, brethren, that flesh and blood cannot inherit the kingdom of God; neither doth corruption inherit incorruption."

We become spiritual by being born again of the word and the Spirit of God and by continually feeding the spirit man with the word of God. The more we feed on the word of God spiritually and have fellowship with God in prayer and meditating upon the word of God we grow spiritually, and we start to operate in the kingdom of God, we are ushered into the miraculous supernatural nature of the kingdom. Growing in the kingdom of God is not measured by the number of years that you have been in the church, it's measured by how you have been dealing with the word of God. The key to the kingdom of God is the word. Many people who go to church are just church members, but they are not in the kingdom of God, the church is not the kingdom of God. The church is there to help you get into the kingdom of God by teaching you the word of God. The best example is Nicodemus he was a big man a ruler of the Jews, but he was not in the kingdom of God, and he did not have any understanding of the kingdom of God. You may know the traditions of your church but that does not help you in your growth in the kingdom of God.

When you are in the kingdom of God the word of God starts to affect your life, progressive changes start to happen, your mindset is transformed, and your world view changes. You are given kingdom power and authority as you learn who you are and your position in Christ from the word of God. Signs and wonders start to follow you. Mark 16:17 -18 [17] And these signs shall follow them that believe; In my name shall they cast out devils; they shall speak with new tongues; [18] They shall take up serpents; and they if drink any deadly thing, it shall not hurt them; they shall lay hands on the sick, and they shall recover."

Isaiah 54:17 "No weapon that is formed against thee shall prosper; and every tongue that shall rise against thee in judgement thou shalt condemn.

This is the heritage of the servants of the Lord, and their righteousness is of me, saith the Lord." As one gets rooted in the word of God you get understanding of the negative effects of sin upon your life and you feel the urge to stop living in sin and eventually you pursue holiness and righteousness. 1 John 3:8-10 [8] "He that committeth sin is of the devil; for the devil sinneth from the beginning. For this purpose the son of God was manifested, that he might destroy the works of the devil.[9] Whosoever is born of God doth not commit sin; for his seed remaineth in him: and he cannot sin, because he is born of God. [10] In this the children of God are manifest, and the children of the devil: whosoever doeth not righteousness is not of God, neither he that loveth not his brother." When you are in the kingdom of God you live eternally and eternal life is the life of God, you pursue righteousness, you live according to the word of God.

The power of the kingdom of God and the word of God will turn you into another man. This is a sign that you must watch for, you cannot remain the same person when you are in the kingdom of God. 1 Samuel 10:6 "And the Spirit of the Lord will come upon thee, and thou shalt prophesy with them, and shalt be turned into another man." The kingdom of God comes to you with new life, if you cannot see new life both spiritually and physically it means the kingdom of God is not yet in you.

You come to know and to understand the dynamics of the kingdom of God through the word of God through the power of the Holy Spirit. When the word of God is at work in you through the Holy Spirit, you receive revelation. Revelation is when the Holy Spirit is imparting knowledge to you supernaturally about the things of God. Revelation is having knowledge freely from God without going to a formal school where you must spend many years trying to learn a discipline. God gives his children knowledge of the kingdom freely. Matthew 8:8 "Heal the sick, cleanse the lepers, raise the dead, cast out devils: freely ye have received, freely give." John 14:26 "But the comforter, which is the Holy Ghost, whom the Father will send in my name, he shall teach you all things, and bring all things to your remembrance, whatsoever I have said unto you." Revelation makes the kingdom of God real because you are seeing things with your spiritual eyes. What the word of God says is made real by revelation. Without revelation you cannot know

God and the kingdom of God it is not real. During the days of Jesus when he was walking on this earth people saw him physically but still, they did not know who he really was. Matthew 16:13-17 [13] When Jesus came into coasts of Caesarea Philippi, he asked his disciples, saying, Whom do men say that I the Son of man am? [14] And they said, Some say that thou art John the Baptist: some, Elias; and others, Jeremias, or one of the prophets. [15] He saith unto them, But whom say ye that I am? [16] And Simon Peter answered and said, Thou art the Christ, the Son of the living God. [17] And Jesus answered and said unto him, Blessed art thou, Simon Bar-Jona: for flesh and blood hath not revealed it unto thee, but my Father which is in heaven." You need revelation to know Jesus Christ and the things of the kingdom of God. Although the disciples were living with Jesus Christ, they still needed revelation to know him. Even today you may read from scriptures about him but unless you get revelation from the word by the Holy Spirit, you cannot know him. You must see him spiritually because he is spirit otherwise you are just following what you do not know.

We appropriate what belongs to us in the kingdom of God by the word of God and his Spirit. John 6:63 "It is the spirit that quickeneth; the flesh profiteth nothing: the words that I speak unto you, they are spirit, and they are life." If you ignore His word, you will get nothing from the Kingdom of God. You must obey God from the spiritual point of view, not from the flesh's point of view. When you obey spiritually the Holy Spirit helps us to obey and he empowers us to obey, you do not choose on what to obey but you obey everything that God instructs you to do. There is joy in obeying God from the spiritual point of view but obeying from the fleshly point of view it is a very heavy burden and it takes away joy, it is difficult and impossible.

You operate in the kingdom of God with your spirit. Operating with your flesh does not work because your flesh is fallen and limited already. John 3: 6 "That which is born of the flesh is flesh; and that which is born of the spirit is spirit." You are a spirit with a spiritual body living in a physical body therefore, you should be operating from the spiritual realm. The reason why you are not excited of the things of God it is because you are using your physical body to do the things of the spirit. Galatians 5:17 "For the flesh lusteth against the Spirit, and the Spirit against the flesh: and these are contrary the one to the other: so that ye cannot do the things that ye would." Your body has not yet been saved it is still interested in sinning, it was born in iniquity. Psalm 51:5 "Behold, I was sharpen in iniquity; and in sin did my mother conceive me."

The flesh cannot understand the things of God, it does not matter how much you can force yourself to do the things of God the flesh cannot do spiritual things. The flesh operates from a different dimension from that of the spirit. When you are not yet born again your spirit is dead and inactive. It can only be raised from the dead by the word of God and the spirit of God. Many times, unregenerated men and women engage in some breakthrough prayers trying to get results out of those prayers yet they will be praying in the flesh because their spirits are dead. There is no breakthrough because they will be trying to do things that are beyond the scope of their flesh. Your mind and body are meant to operate in this physical world and not in the spiritual world or the kingdom of God.

The promises of God that we find in the word of God they are hidden in your spirit. You get them out of your spirit by the word of God and by the power of the Holy Spirit. You get things out of your spirit by faith. Faith is the ability to hear from God and see what God is doing in the spiritual realm and you believe it and accept then it will be manifested in your life. If you see nothing in your spirit, then you will get nothing. You cannot live above what you see from your spirit. You do not do what you want to do in the kingdom of God obey the king of the kingdom. Romans 6:16 "Know ye not, that to whom ye yield yourselves servants to obey, his servants ye are to whom ye obey; whether of sin unto death, or of obedience unto righteousness?" The righteousness of God is key in the kingdom of God not your righteousness. You have the righteousness of Christ; without the word of God you will lose this righteousness.

You continue in the word of God for you to continue living in his righteousness. Romans 5:17 "For if by one man's offense death reigned by one; much more they which receive abundance of grace and the gift of righteousness shall reign in life by one, Jesus Christ." You cannot earn the righteousness of God it is a gift given to you through Christ, but what you can do is to keep it. If I do not live according to the word of God, you will lose it. Ephesians 2:8 "For by grace are ye saved through faith; and that not of yourselves: it is the gift of God." What has been given to you as a gift it is your responsibility to keep it.

12

The Word of God is Spirit and Life.

John 6:63 "It is the spirit that quickeneth; the flesh profiteth nothing: the words that I speak unto you, they are spirit, and they are life." The word of God without the Holy Spirit does not work, it is empowered by the Holy Spirit, therefore it is paramount for every believer to be filled by the Holy Spirit, so that when he speaks the word of God that word goes out filled with the power of the Holy Spirit. The word will then go out and accomplish that which it has been sent to do. Isiah 55:11 "So shall my word be that goeth forth out of my mouth:it shall not return void, but it shall accomplish that which I please, and shall prosper in the thing whereto I sent it." With the Holy Spirit, the word of God works in different forms to achieve different things as we are going to see in this chapter.

The word of God is not one thing it is many things, it operates

DYNAMICS OF THE WORD OF GOD!! | 61

in many different ways:

1. The word of God can work like a sword. Hebrews 4:12 "For the word of God is quick, and powerful, and sharper than any two-edged sword, piercing even to the dividing asunder of soul and spirit, and of the joints and marrow, and is a discerner of the thoughts and intents of the heart." The word of God is a weapon that you use to defend yourself through the Holy Spirit. It is also a weapon you can use to be offensive with in the world of darkness.

2. It is like fire and like a hammer. Jeremiah 23:29 "Is not my word like as fire? saith the lord; and like a hammer that breaketh the rock into pieces? There are things in your life that needs to be burnt by the fire of the word of God and some that need to be broken by the hammer of the word of God. There may be some generational curses, iniquities, and sins in your life they need the word of God to be destroyed. Being born again is the initial stage of our deliverance it must continue with the word of God. The generational curses do not disappear on the day we get born again they continue with you that is why you need the word of God to deal with those curses as you continue working out your own salvation. Without the word of God, there is no change of life both physically and spiritually that can be witnessed. Philippians 2:12 "Wherefore, my beloved, as ye have always obeyed, not in my presence only, but in my absence, work out your own salvation with fear and trembling." Many children of God do not understand that every change in your life as a child of God comes by the word of God.

3. The word of God is like a mirror. James 1:22 -24 [22] "But be ye doers of the word, and not hearers only, deceiving your own selves. [23] For if any be a hearer of the word, and not a doer, he is like unto a man beholding his natural face in a glass: [24], For he beholdeth himself, and goeth his way, and straightway forgetteth what manner of man he was." The word of God shows you what must do, it shows you where you are not good the same way a mirror shows you how you look like. The word of God shows you the real you not what you are not, therefore you must not ignore it. Correct the things that are being shown to you. Many Christians choose and pick the verses that they want to study those that talk about their greatness in God only but ignore those verses that rebuke and correct them.

4. It is like rain. Isaiah 55:10 -11 [10] "For as the rain cometh down, and the snow from heaven, and returneth not hither, but watereth the earth, and maketh it bring forth and bud, that it may give seed to the sower, and bread to the eater: [11] So shall my word be that goeth forth out of my mouth: it shall not return to me void, but it shall accomplish that which I please, and it shall prosper in the thing whereto I sent it." Rain brings life to everything so does the word of God give you life. The word brings transformation in the lives of the children of God and ignoring the word is ignoring your life.

Everything new in your life is brought by the word. All the dead life that is in you that you got when Adam and Eve disobeyed God is brought back to life by the word of God. There is no way that your life can become fruitful without the word of God. Genesis 1:28 " And God blessed them,and God said unto them, be fruitful, and multiply, and replenish the earth, and subdue it: and have dominion over the fish of the sea, and over the fowl of the air, and over every living thing that moveth upon the earth." Some think that prayer is the only thing that can change lives. Prayer that you do outside the word of God is useless and does not work. Without rain everything dries up in the world and without the word of God in your life everything dries up. The word of God waters the life that is already in you and it starts to flourish, to be fruitful.

5. The word of God is the bread of life. John 6:35 "And Jesus said unto them, I am the bread of life: he that cometh to me shall never hunger; and he that believeth on me shall never thirsty." The way that you are nourished by bread naturally that is how the word of God nourishes you spiritually. How you get strength from natural bread that is how you get spiritual strength from the word of God.

Many children of God are spiritually starving because they do not have time to feed their spirits by the word of God. Many have starved themselves to death spiritually, but they are still going to church. They still call themselves children of God, but they can no longer even hear from their Father God. You can still think all is well with you as you are doing many things in your church and you are loved by all but if you are ignoring the word of God you are very miserable and you are heading for a very big disaster in your life.

6. It is like seed. Luke 8:5-11. [5] "A sower went out to sow his seed: and as he sowed, some fell by the wayside; and it was trodden down, and the fowls of the air devoured it. [6] And some fell upon a rock;and as soon as it was sprung up, it withered away, because it lacked moisture. [7] And some fell among thorns; and the thorns sprang up with it, and choked it. [8] And other fell on good ground, and sprang up, and bare fruit a hundredfold. And when he had said these things, he cried, He that hath ears to hear, let him hear."

The word of God is seed; it must be planted into your spirit, your spirit is the good fertile ground. When the word of God gets into your spirit it produces life in you. Life starts to germinate in you, the blessings of God that are in you in your spirit man starts to flourish. God has put everything that you need in your life in your spirit. Your spirit is like an egg that is in the womb of a woman. When that egg is fertilized by the seed of a man she conceives and later gives birth to a baby. This is how it works spiritually as well. When the word of God gets it your spirit you conceive spiritually and later you produce life, you produce the blessings of God that are in you. If you do not have the word of God, you are like a sterile man who is not able to impregnate his wife.

Therefore, if nothing is happening in your life do not blame God it is your fault you are failing to fertilize what is in you by the seed of the word of God. The earth has got potential to produce anything that is planted in it. It is the same with your spirit it is like the earth when you plant the seed of the word your spirit can produce all the life that has been put in it by God when you were created.

7. The word of God is like water. John 15:3 "Now ye are clean through the word which I have spoken unto you." We need spiritual cleansing in the same manner that we need cleansing with natural water every day of our lives. We need water to drink and to clean ourselves. The word of God must do the same to the spirit man that has been born of God. Children of God ignore the word of God and yet everything is centered on that word in the kingdom of God. The kingdom of God is a spiritual kingdom, but we cannot experience its spirituality if we ignore the word of God, God does everything by his word. Jeremiah 1:12 "Then said the Lord unto me, Thou hast well seen: for I will hasten my word to perform it."

13

The Word of God is universal, permanent, and ignoring it brings judgement

Matthew 24:35 "Heaven and earth shall pass away, but my words shall not pass away." The word of God works anywhere and for everyone if only one believes in God who is the word. John 1:1 "In the beginning was the word, and the word was with God, and the word was God."
I have seen people move from country to country in search of a good life. You do not need to move to another country seeking a better life. If you believe in the word of God and you do what it says you will have better life wherever you are. People say they are relocating to greener pastures. There are no greener pastures in this world, God can transform your life wherever you are if you just believe in him.

Isaac dwelt in Gerar and it happened that there was a famine in the land Isaac sowed and he received hundredfold. The word of God says that he became very rich until he grew very rich. I am saying to confirm to you that what you need most for you to prosper in your life is God. The word of God also says that it is the blessing of the Lord that makes you rich. Hard work is good but above that you need the blessing of the Lord wherever you are. Genesis 26:12 [12] "Then Isaac sowed in that land, and received in the same year a hundredfold: and the Lord blessed him.[13] And the man waxed great, and went forward, and grew until he became very great." The word of God does not work in certain nations and does not work in other nations.

I have come across many people who think that they need to go to Europe or America for their lives to change they think God cannot change them in Africa. This is very sad indeed, the word of God has no geographical location for it to work, it works everywhere if you just believe. The word of God guar- antees prosperity and success. Joshua 1:8 "This book of the law shall not depart out of thy mouth; but thou shalt meditate therein day and night, that thou mayest observe to do according to all that is written therein: for then thou shalt make thy way prosperous, and then thou shalt have good success." If one believes in the word of God, he cannot fail at any time. The word of God is a sure foundation that you can build your life upon, and you will never regret it. Children of God know the word of God, but that word is not related to most of their lives, the word of God is taking its own course and their lives are taking another course. The word of God is spoken in church and put into songs that are sung with all the passion but after the church service, people live lives that have nothing to do with that word.

The law or the word of God if broken, has got many consequences, it has inherent judgement in it. The more you break the law or the word of God the more you are automatically judged. You may not see the judgement there and then but sooner or later the consequences will catch up with you even with your posterity. Ecclesiastes 8:11 -13 [11]

"Because sentences against an evil work is not executed speedily, therefore the heart of the sons of men is fully set in them to do evil.[12] Though a sinner do evil an hundred times, and his days be prolonged, yet I surely know that it shall be well with them that fear God, which fear before him:[13] But it shall not be well with the wicked, neither shall he prolong his days, which are as a shadow; because he feareth not before God." Deuteronomy 5:9 "Thou shalt not bow down thyself unto them, nor serve them; for I, the Lord thy God, am a jealous God, visiting the iniquity of the fathers upon children unto the third and fourth generation of them that hate me." People are suffering in the world because they ignore the word of God, and they do what they want.

The world is suffering today because Adam and Eve did not obey the word of God, you were not there but you are having the consequences of their disobedience. Some think that when they disobey God, God will wait to judge them on the final judgement. That is why it is called final judgement it is so because there are other judgements that you suffer now before you face the final judgement. Here and now, you are not being judged by Christ, but you are being judged by the word of God itself because within it if you disobey it, it judges you. On the final judgement day, you are going to be judged by Christ himself.

Many things that people are going through here on earth are judgements because they disobey the word of God. I said earlier that this world is physical, but it is spiritual at the same time because it came out of the spiritual world, and it is run by spiritual laws. The spiritual laws are the word of God. If you break any law in this world, you suffer for it even in your city if break certain laws you get yourself in trouble. If you overspeed you will get a ticket, that is the judgement of the law that you have broken.

14

The purposes of the word of God

If children of God do not take heed the devil is always distracting them from studying the word of God so that they cannot get its benefits. It is easy to substitute the studying of the word of God with religious activities. The Apostles in the New Testament new the importance of the word of God. They had to give themselves continually to prayer and the ministry of the word of God. Acts 6:2,4 [2] "Then the twelve called the multitude of the disciples unto them, and said, it is not reason that we should leave the word of God and serve tables. [4] But we will give ourselves continually to prayer, and to the ministry of the word." Prosperity and success were promised to Joshua by God, but it was all in the word of God. The way he handled the word of God determined his prosperity and success. He instructed firstly that the book of the law was not supposed to depart out of his mouth, he was to stay in the word of God. Secondly, he was to meditate upon it day and night, meaning all the time. Thirdly he had to practice the word of God. He had to live the word. Joshua 1:8 "This book of the law shall not depart out of thy mouth; but thou shalt meditate therein day and night, that thou mayest observe to do according to all that is written therein: for then thou shalt make thy way prosperous, and then thou shalt have good success.

From the above we can see that Joshua oversaw his prosperity and success, it was all up to him he had to make a choice. If he ignored the instructions of God, he was going to fail. It is also true for us today if we are in the kingdom of God there is no way that we are going to prosper or succeed if we ignore the word of God. Everything that God does he does it through his word, ignoring his word is ignoring him. You are failing because you are failing to live by the word of God. You stumble because you walk in darkness, the word of God is light to your feet. Psalm 119:105 "Thy word is a lamp unto my feet, and a light to my path."

Life is hidden in the word of God, but many people put their trust in other people for their lives to change. Change is in God and his word. Success and prosperity do not come as an instantaneous miracle, but it is progressive. For this progression to start happening you must decide to stay in the word of God all the time not sometimes, and you must dig deeper. Your prosperity and success are locked up in your spirit man. Proverbs 4:23 "Keep thy heart with all diligence; for out of it are the issues of life." The word of God through the power of the Holy Spirit is the key that unlocks it. Genesis 1:27-28 "So God created man in his own image, in the image of God created he him; male and female created he them.[28] And God blessed them,and God said unto them Be fruitful, and multiply, and replenish the earth, and subdue it: and have dominion over the fish of the sea, and over the fowl of the air,and over every living thing that moveth upon the earth." Without the word of God what has been put in you by God will never manifest itself in your life, you will die with it.

Dr Myles Munroe says that the richest place on earth is the cemetery because people die with many things in them without using not even a single thing or blessing that God put in them when he created them.

The word of God gives you a strong relationship with God and you understand the mind of God and who he is by his word. Psalm 119:104 "Through thy precepts I get understanding: therefore, I hate every false way." His thoughts and his ways are only known through his word. His character and his promises to us are only known through his word. His relationship and love of the world is made clear in his word. God's dealings with the world are revealed in his word. The word of God is food to the spirit man. It is not studied to make arguments. 2 Timothy 2: 15-16 [15] "Study to show thyself approved unto God, a workman that needeth not to be ashamed, rightly dividing the word of truth.[16] But shun profane and vain bubblings: for they will increase unto more ungodliness."

You study it to nourish the spirit man that is in you who is the real you, as you might know that you are three in one, soul, spirit, and body. Your soul comprises of your emotions, intellect, senses, your body is your flesh and spirit that is the part that is spiritual that understands the things of God. That is where Christ resides when you get born again and that is the part that gets born again not your body and your soul. Your spirit is the part that was created in the image of God, it has the DNA of God

The word of God is not for show off and it is not magic, it is God himself. Some people think that they can just use the word of God to acquire material things and to get physical healing. The word of God is not as cheap as all that. Unless you are saved born again the word of God does not work to those who are not his children. You must be spiritually skilful for you to be able to use the word of God. Without having the Holy Spirit in you, you are not skilful enough, it is the Holy Spirit who gives you skill.

Jesus Christ is only formed in you by the word of God. Galatians 4:19 "My little children, of whom I travail in birth again until Christ be formed in you," Without the word of God you cannot be like Christ and being like Christ gives us the authority of Christ as we live in this world. Christs make us to be able to live above everything in this world, he was above everything in the world. Just memorizing scriptures without living them only makes you to be a religious person without the power of God. Demons know all the scriptures, but they live the opposite of what scriptures say. James 2:19-20 [19] "Thou believest that there is one God; thou doest well: the devils also believe, and tremble. [20] But wilt thou know, O vain man, that faith without works is dead?"

Worshipping God is all about Christ being formed in us. If Christ is not formed in us by the word of God, we cannot operate in the kingdom of God. When he is formed you get the ability to deal with situations that confront you the same way Christ did. Matthew 8:25 -26 [25] "And his disciples came to him, and awoke him saying Lord, save us: we perish, [26] And he saith unto them, Why are ye fearful, O ye of little faith? Then he arose, and rebuked the winds and the sea; and there was a great calm.[27] But the men marvelled, saying.

What manner of man is this, that even the winds and the sea obey him!" This is the desire of God for you to live like him, you are his child therefore you must live like him. When Christ is formed in you as a child of God you get the mindset of Christ, you start to think like him. Philippians 2:5 "Let this mind be in you, which was also in Christ Jesus." Without the word of God, you continue to live with your old unregenerated mindset and as a result nothing that has been promised by God in his word will ever happen in your life.

The children of Israel were delivered by God from Egypt but they continued living in Egypt in their minds, yet they had gone out of it. They did not embrace the new life that God had given them. Transformation of your life comes as renew your mind by the word of God, Romans 12:2 "And be not conformed to this world: but be ye transformed by the renewing of your mind, that ye may prove what is that good, and acceptable, and perfect, will of God." When Christ is formed in us through his word, we get the same world view with him. Jeremiah 5:21 "Hear now this, O foolish people, and without understanding; which have eyes, and see not; which have ears, and hear not." When he is formed in you then he will be manifested in you, and you will have his nature.

When you have his nature, you start to walk like him, and see the world with his eyes. You will see yourself with the eyes of God, understand your purpose on earth and who you are. You will start to perceive and understand your destiny, your priorities in life change you will have the same priorities with God. You start to understand people better because the more you understand God the more you understand other people, people hold a special place in God.

Once you have the nature of God every material thing is attracted to you because everything was created by God. Matthew 6:33 "But seek ye first the kingdom of God, and his righteousness; and all these things shall be added unto you." The blessing of Abraham that you get through Christ does not work with the old nature it only works with the new nature. Many people want the blessing of Abraham and yet they are doing nothing in getting the nature of God. Yes, you get the nature of God when we get born again but that nature does not work until it is made to work by the word of God. Philippians 2:12 "Wherefore, my beloved, as ye have always obeyed, not as in my presence only, but now much more in my presence only, work out your own salvation with fear and trembling." The blessing of Abraham is only attracted to the nature of God.

How you grow in the new nature that is how you grow in the blessing of Abraham. Many people just think that if they give to God that is how God is going to give back to them. God rewards those who have developed themselves to have his nature, it is not about giving only. Many times, when you give without his nature you give for wrong reasons. You give to God being pushed by carnal desires. The blessings of God come to you as you grow in his nature. Your old nature is cursed, and your new nature carries the blessing of God, therefore come out of the old nature, and develop your new nature. The godly you become the more closer you are moving to the blessing of Abraham.

We are born into the supernatural kingdom of God by his word. 1 Peter 1:23 "Being born again, not of corruptible seed, but of incorruptible, by the word of God, which liveth and abideth for ever." John 3:16 "That which is born of the flesh is flesh; and that which is born of the spirit is spirit." The word of God gives us the supernatural nature of God. You cannot pray for people to get healed if you do not have this supernatural nature of God. Mark 16:17 -18 [17} And these signs shall follow them that believe; in my name shall they cast out devils; they shall speak with new tongues; [18] They shall take up serpents; and if they drink any deadly thing, it shall not hurt them; they shall lay hands on the sick, and they shall recover." The supernatural nature that is in you causes signs and wonders, miracles to follow your life. Faith is created in your spirit and not in your natural mind by the word of God. Your natural mind is only a passage of the word of God into your spirit.

If the word does not proceed into your spirit, you cannot have the faith of God working. Romans 10:17 "So then faith cometh by hearing, and hearing by the word of God" Many people think they have spiritual faith, yet their faith is just natural faith, the faith that you need as a child of God is spiritual faith. It is the word of God that you have understood spiritually and that has produced faith in you that will bring a difference in your life.

When the word of God gets into your spirit it produces revelation and revelation produces faith. The word of God that you speak from the mind does not have power. You must speak the word of God that is coming from your spirit man filled with the power of the Holy Spirit that word is powerful and it brings results Hebrews 4:12 " For the word of God is quick, and powerful,and sharper than any twoedged sword, piercing even to the dividing asunder of soul and spirit, and of the joints and marrow, and is a discerner of the thought and intents of the heart." Job 22:28 "Thou shalt also decree a thing and it shall be established unto thee: and the light shall shine upon thy ways." No disease or situation can resist the power of the word when it is coming out of the spirit of a man by the power of the Holy Spirit.

The word of God destroys strongholds in our lives. 2 Corithians 10:4 -5 [4] For the weapons of our warfare are not canal, but mighty through God to the pulling down of strongholds. [5] Casting down imaginations, and every high thing that that exalts itself against the knowledge of God and bringing into captivity every thought to the obedience of christ;" Strongholds are doctrines that are against the word of God that we have been taught from the time that we were born upon which our lives are built upon.

The lives of the people in the world are built upon the lies of the devil and these are strongholds. It is only the word of God that can set us free from these strongholds. John 8: 31 -32 [31] Then Jesus said to those Jews which believed on him, if ye continue in my word, then are ye my disciples; indeed, And ye shall know the truth, and the truth shall make you free." Strongholds are always holding you back in your life, you want to advance but strongholds resist you. Strongholds are built in your mind by the wrong teachings doctrines of demons that you were exposed from the time you were born. These strongholds are buit by demons and the devil, they are even stronger than demons. After you cast out demons from someone and you do not destroy strongholds in his life the demons will still come back because they are attracted by them.

Matthew 12:43 -45 [43] "When the unclean spirit is gone out of a man, he walketh through dry places, seeking rest, and findeth none.[44] Then he saith, I will return into my house from whence I came out; and when he is come, findeth it empty, swept and garnished. [45] Then goeth he, and taketh with himself seven other spirits more wicked than himself, and they enter in and dwell there: and the last state of that man is worse than the first. Even so shall it be also unto this wicked generation."

The word of God has power through the Holy Spirit to destroy strongholds. Jeremiah 23:29 "Is not my word like as a fire?saith the lord; and like a hammer that breaketh the rock in pieces?" We do not get transformed by God through our spiritual gifts. We are transformed by the word of God. As an individual you do not benefit much from your spiritual gift, but it is other people. Therefore, do not get carried away by your spiritual gift and yet you are not working out your life by the word of God. This is why you find some Pastors they can preach very good sermons about getting out of poverty and yet they are still in poverty. Those hearing him can come out of poverty but if he does nothing with the word of God to fight poverty, he will continue in it.

15

Spirit of poverty.

Poverty is in many different areas of our lives eg there is spiritual poverty, relational poverty, emotional poverty, marital poverty, and financial poverty, etc. I have just given a few examples. Poverty means not having enough, or lacking. Google says "the state of being extremely poor. The state of being inferior in quality or insufficient in amount." Poverty is a spiritual state which causes someone to lack. When someone has this spirit, he is empowered to lack, everything he tries to do to change his situation is resisted by some unforeseen forces. The source of poverty is the devil, when you have this spirit everything you try to acquire is destroyed somehow. Poverty is the opposite of being blessed, a blessed man lives a life of abundance, and he is empowered to prosper by God. The spirit of poverty causes you to struggle in everything that you try to do.

The spirit of poverty is the devil himself. John 10:10 "The thief cometh not, but to steal, and to kill, and to destroy: I am come that they might have life, and that they might have it more abundantly." After you are born again you are taken out of this spirit by the death and resurrection of Christ but if you do not use the word of God you will continue to live under this spirit. You must be serious with the word of God otherwise nothing is going to change. This is a major problem with many children of God. They get carried away by church activities and programs but ignore the word of God. The church cannot transform you even your Pastor, what transforms you and brings abundance is the word of God.

The bible says it is the blessing of God that makes us rich. How do you get the blessing, by living in obedience to the word of God? Without the word of God, we cannot obey God. Abraham was blessed by God because he lived a life of obedience, and that obedience brought the blessing of God. We only get the blessing by obedience to his word. Genesis 22:12 "And he said, lay not thine hand upon the lad, neither do thou anything unto him: for now I know that thou fearest God, seeing thou hast not withheld thy son, thine only son from me." When I came to the Lord many years ago, I thought poverty was just going to leave me automatically since I had been born again. The preachers also by then used to say if you are saved just wait the blessings of God are going to come to you. So, I waited but doing nothing and nothing happened to me.

I got frustrated because my life was not changing, I thank God who then revealed to me that God could not change my life unless I agreed with him that his word is true and that it can change my life if live what it says. God started to reveal to me the importance of the word and I started to see spiritually that all that I needed was all in the word of God. This is what has pushed me to write this book to help someone who thinks that change is going to come in his life because she goes to a certain church with powerful preachers. It is good to go to church but you must major in the word of God yourself, your Pastor cannot do that for you. I had to believe the word of God and live that which I believed myself not someone else on my behalf. To study and to live the word of God is not a small job it is a very big task that is why very few people do it but that is where real life is found. Poverty is not a dead thing, it is a living thing, it is the devil himself you must fight him with something that is also alive and that is the word of God. If you are only faithful to your church but not faithful to the word of God you will be faithfully very poor indeed.

At Calvary Christ empowered us to be able to come out of poverty and he gave us weapons to use to come of it. One of the weapons is the word of God, unfortunately, this weapon is not being used. The spirit of poverty closes the eyes of your spiritual mind so that you cannot see opportunities and you are always seeing negative things where others see opportunities. For example, someone might say to you why don't you open a shop, and you say there are too many shops in our area. You always see the negative and not the positive. To come out of poverty, I mean every type of poverty as I alluded to earlier that you must prosper spiritually first.

The desire of God is for us to prosper in everything that is the reason he came to die on the cross. Prosperity is hidden in the word of God. 3 John1:2 "Beloved, I wish above all things that thou mayest proper and be in health, even as thy soul prospereth." The soul being referred to in this verse is the spirit, your spirit. The prosperity of your spirit is key to all other successes and prosperity. You need to prosper first and foremost in your relationship with your father God. The spirit cannot prosper without the word of God, and this is where the rubber meets the road many Christians want to prosper in their lives but do not feed their spirits with the word of God. They think they can prosper by being prayed for by the Pastor, if the Pastor prays for you but inside of you, you are empty of the word nothing happens. A pastor's prayer or anointing must meet with the word that has been planted in you.

If there is nothing of the word of God happening in you which I call spiritual activity then there is no change from God taking place in your life. Your spirit is the powerhouse for change and that powerhouse is fueled by the word of God. Spiritual activity in your life is caused by the word of God that you have in your spirit not in your mind by the power of the Holy Spirit. As child of God, all your changes start from within you and is manifested outwardly. Spiritual activity steers the life that is in you so that it becomes fruitful. This is how you come out of poverty. You do not come out of poverty by just fasting and doing breakthrough prayer but without the word of God in you. You can go ahead and pray and fast but sooner or later you shall get tired and stop it.

I have seen and I have also attended conferences and these prayers where you are being told to do certain things that are not scriptural even being asked to give money to God so that you may come out of poverty, it does not work that way. Stay in the word do what it says, and you will come out of poverty step by step. Prayer and fasting are good but they must be done in line with the word of God.

16

The mindset of Jesus Christ.

Philippians 2:5 "Let this mind be in you, which was also in Christ Jesus.

Christians get defeated by the enemy the devil sometimes, the reason is not that they do not pray, it is because they pray with a wrong mindset. Your prayers are regulated by your mindset, if you have a wrong mind- set normally you pray amiss. You may know verses mentally, but that word does not change your mindset. The word that is in your spirit is the one that can change your mindset to give you the mindset of Christ. You must have the mind of Christ to pray effectively and according to the will of God. What is a mindset? Here are some definitions from Google, "The established set of attitudes held by someone as a result of what he has gone through, his environment, what he has been taught, what he has seen people doing in society that he grew up in." "A mindset is a set of beliefs that shape how you make sense of the world and yourself. It influences how you think, feel, and behave in any given situation." "A mindset is a series of self-perceptions or beliefs people hold about themselves. These determine behaviour, outlook, and mental attitude."

The mindset gives a person his scope of thinking and their opinions. It is the pattern of your thinking, and it is a fixed state of mind. There are factors that causes you to think the way you think. The factors are beliefs, doctrines, education and what you have gone through in life. Psalm 51:5 "behold, I was born in iniquity, and in sin did my mother conceive me." Every man is a product of how he thinks, and he cannot live above how you thinks. Your mindset affects your character as well. The only way that can have the mindset of Christ is when you consistently and persistently expose yourself spiritually to the word of God. Our old mindset cannot operate or work in the kingdom of God. 2 Corinthians 5:17 "Therefore if any man be in Christ, he is a new creature: old things are passed away; behold all things are become new." We only become new as we change our mindset. Things become new as our mindsets are renewed by the word of God.

It does not matter the powerful teachers of the word of God that you may have unless your mindset gets changed by those teachings you will not get better in life. Before you change the way, you do things your mindset must change first. You are what you are because of your mindset, and the good news is that you can change your mindset. Study the word of God and live that word as you do that through the power of the Holy Spirit your mindset will change step by step. When you get born again what which gets born again is your spirit man and you do not get the mind- set of Christ automatically. You must acquire the mindset of Christ by the word of God and his spirit.

Changing your mindset does not take a miracle to happen and it is not a day job, it is an ongoing undertaking, this is the biggest problem that is in the church the saints are busy running up and down and they do not have time for the word of God hence they continue with their old world." Things of the kingdom of God are accessed by the mindset of Christ. The devil is creating activity pressure in the world to distract the saints from meditating upon the word of God. When your mind is not settled it is very hard to sit and study the word of God. Understanding the deeper things of God demands a steady mind. People spend all their time in worldly dealings and hence they develop a worldly mindset instead of the mindset of Christ.

What is binding you is within you, and what sets you free is within you as well. The mindset that you have either binds you or it makes you free. The devil binds you by giving you his mindset through his lies and God sets you free by giving you his mindset through his word. Without the word of God there is no way you can be free from the grip of the devil. Jesus has made Christians kings and priests but because they do not have the mindset of Christ many are living as slaves. Revelation 1:6 "And hath made us kings and priests unto God and his Father; to him be glory and dominion for ever and ever. Amen." You must have the mindset of a king to live like a king, it is impossible to have a mindset of a slave and live like a king.

Many times, Christians complain and say things are not changing in their lives, God is not changing them. If you do not have the mindset of Christ, you cannot see a change in your life. Change in your life comes as your way of thinking changes. The bible says as a man thinks in his heart that is what he becomes. If you continue to think like the devil or just as a natural man, you cannot get any change in your life from God and that is not the problem of God. Preachers of the word of God let us empower people and help them develop the mindset of Jesus Christ because this is what brings transformation in their lives.

You cannot change people by any other means. Ephesians 4:11 -12 [11] "And he gave some, apostles, and some, prophets; and some evangelists;

and some pastors and teachers;[12] For the perfecting of the saints, for the work of the ministry, for the edifying of the body of Christ:" The perfecting of the saints is for the saints to have the mindset of Jesus Christ. Many times, you as a preacher you think you can change them by laying your hands upon them and that is what they also believe but that is not correct.

If Christians do not have the mind of Christ, they put their trust for their change in their Pastor or leader instead of God. Today in some places in the world we are seeing some Pastors getting some satanic powers so that they may seem to be bringing change in the lives of the people that they are leading. God has never given his power to change another man to another man if he could do this it would have created so many problems. Those with that power would abuse and misuse it and some people would end up not being changed, therefore God remains with that power in his word so that every individual is able to access it.

Saints are being misled because they are not aware that the changes, they are looking for are not in other human beings. The changes are within you use the word of God and his Spirit and your life will never be same again. You do not need to buy air tickets to go to a far away countrie everything is within you. God is very fair he has put everything within your reach so that no one could say to him I failed to get money to go to where change is found. Many are lazy to search for the truth from the scriptures themselves they want shortcuts to reach to their destinies.

David managed to kill Goliath not because of the weapons that he had, but because of his mindset. He saw his ability in God not in himself and he also saw the ability of Goliath against that of his God. He knew that it was not him fighting with Goliath but his God therefore, he was ready to engage in a fight with Goliath. Saul and all his soldiers ran away from the same Goliath because of their mindset, they did not see God in everything that was happening they just saw themselves against Goliath, they sized everything that the enemy had, and they saw themselves as very inferior to him and hence were not able to engage in a fight with him.

Spend time with God in his word and you will develop the mindset of Christ. Proverbs 13:20 "He that walketh with wise men shall be wise; but a companion of fools shall be destroyed." Without the mind of Christ which is a spiritual mind you cannot develop the character of God. The world has the character of the devil because it has the mindset of the devil. Feeding the spirit man with the word of God develops the mind of Christ. Your destiny and the blessings of God are connected to your spiritual mind, the mind of Christ.

17

Spiritual Authority

Jesus has authority and you must have authority as a child of God because you live in him and him in you. Matthew 28:18 "And Jesus came and spoke unto them, saying, all power is given unto me in heaven and in earth." When you get born again, you are given a measure of authority, but you must develop it and you develop it as you feed on the word of God. This is the reason the devil distracts you when you want to study the word of God. He knows that if you develop and grow in authority, he will not be able to do what he wants with your life. Since you have been made a king by Christ, you need authority to operate as a king. Authority is the power to command. You cannot have authority without developing your character so that you may have the character of Christ. Authority and character are inseparable in the kingdom of God.

How do you get the character of God, you get his character by living the word of God. The more you live like Christ the more authority you then have. You need authority to be able to speak to situations and live above the challenges that are brought into your life by the devil and his demons and the systems that are running the world. Authority is not given to babies, but it is given to mature children of God. Ecclesiastes

10:16 -17 "Woe to thee, O land, when thy king is a child, and thy princes eat in the morning! Blessed art thou, O land, when thy king is the son of nobles, and thy princes eat in due season, for strength, and not for drunkenness!" 1Corinthians 13:11 "When I was a child, I spoke like a child, I thought like a child, reasoned like a child. When I became a man, I gave up childish ways." Sometimes some situations that you are confronted with you do not need to pray as such, but you need to speak a word with authority and situations should change.

When Jesus was in the boat with the disciples when the storm came, he did not pray to God to stop it he spoke authoritatively to it and it stopped. You cannot have authority if you do not understand your position in Jesus Christ. Knowing who you are in Jesus Christ makes you have spiritual authority. To know who you are in Christ and your position in him you must search the scriptures spiritually and get the revelation from the word of God. Elijah was a man like us, but he had spiritual authority which is why he could stop rain for three and half years. James 5:17 -18 [17] Elias was a man subject to like passions as we are, and he prayed earnestly that it might not rain, and it rained not on the earth by the space of three years and six months. [18] And he prayed again, and the heaven gave rain, and the earth brought forth her fruit."

Disobedience to the word of God takes away the authority of God in your life. This is what sin does to you, it takes away authority from you. Authority gives wait to your words when you speak, every demon, and every situation must follow your instructions and commands. Jesus Christ when he was here on earth, he was not operating with spiritual gifts, but he was operating with authority from his life. Spiritual authority is different from the power that Christians have through spiritual gifts. Spiritual gifts operate through the power of the Holy Spirit, but authority works through character and the power of the Holy Spirit. To have a spiritual gift you do not have to have the character of Christ which we get through the word of God. Once you are born again and filled with the Holy Spirit you can have a spiritual gift and start to operate.

Myself I got born again and after three days I was spirit-filled and I started to cast out demons and doing many other great works of power but however, my character was still raw. Nothing had changed in the way that I lived I was still rough with people just as bad as I was before being born again. Spiritual authority comes to you through the help of the Holy Spirit as you work out your character by the word of God. Spiritual gifts can continue to operate even when someone lives in sin, but spiritual authority cannot operate in sin. With spiritual authority, you can decree and declare a thing and it will be established.

Only those with spiritual authority can do this, not all children of God. I have seen people decreeing and declaring and nothing happening and people getting discouraged. Job 22:28 "Thou shalt also decree a thing and it shall be established unto thee: and the light shall shine upon thy ways." Develop your character and have the mindset of Christ then you will be able to do this. If you do not have the mindset and character of Christ and you are granted Spiritual authority you would destroy many innocent souls. You cannot have the mindset of the devil and have the spiritual authority of God it does not work that way.

Abraham because of obedience to the instructions of God through his word attained authority even to bless the families of the whole world. Even after his death, his legacy is still affecting the world today. The blessings of God have become the blessings of Abraham because he was obedient to the word of God. Genesis 12:1-4 "Now the Lord had said unto Abram, Get thee out of thy country, and from thy kindred, and from they father,s house, unto a land that I will shew thee: And I will make of thee a great nation, and I will bless thee, and make thy name great; and thou shalt be a blessin: And I will bless them that bless thee, and curse him that curseth thee: and in thee shall all families of the earth be blessed.

So Abram departed, as the Lord had spoken unto him; and Lot went with him: and Abram was seventy and five years old when he departed out of Haran." God gives wealth to people who have grown spiritually to have spiritual authority. Without the word of God there is no spiritual growth. This is the reason why many Christians just talk about the life of the kingdom of God but they are not living it, they are living in poverty. Proverbs 1: 29 -32 [29] "For that they hated knowledge and did not choose the fear of the Lord: [30] There- fore none of my counsel: they despised all my reproof. [31] Therefore shall they eat of the fruit of their own way and be filled with their own devices.[32] For the turning away of the simple shall slay them, and the prosperity of fools shall destroy them." A person who does not know the ways of God through his word is considered a fool therefore many Christians are fools. They go to church and do all church programs and activities, but they have very little to do with the word of God. For this reason, many are not prospering God is protecting them because as fools if they prosper, they will be destroyed by their prosperity.

Wealth does not come to you through prayer, it comes when you have developed a godly character which in turn brings spiritual authority. Spiritual authority helps you to be able to manage and control the power of wealth. Wealth without spiritual authority will control you and destroy you. Job had spiritual authority, when all of his wealth was destroyed his relationship with his God was never shaken or disturbed. Job 1:20 -22. [20] "Then Job arose, and rent his mantle, and shaved his head, and fell down upon the ground, and worshipped, [21] And said, Naked came I out of my mother's womb, and naked shall I return thither: the Lord gave, and the Lord hath taken away; blessed be the name of the Lord. [22] In all this Job sinned not, nor charged God foolishly." God will not allow wealth to come to you while you are still a fool when you are ignorant of his word.

He loves you so much he does not want you to be destroyed by wealth. He is waiting for you and me to develop spiritually through his word. Mark 8:36 "For what shall it profit a man, if he shall gain the whole world, and lose his own soul?" I hope I have answered this question that is often asked by many Christians, they say why they are not living the abundant kind of life that they read from the word of God. They do not have the capacity to handle abundance because they are fools, he gives wealth to the wise.

The prerequisite for you to be wealthy is having the wisdom of God which gives you spiritual authority.

Adam and Eve when they disobeyed the word of God, they lost all their power and authority in the garden of Eden and they walked away with nothing, they were both naked spiritually and physically. This is what happens to you when we disobey the word of God. Genesis 3:8-11 [8] "And they heard the voice of the Lord God walking in the garden in the cool of the day: and Adam and his wife hid themselves from the presence of the Lord God amongst the trees of the garden, [9] And the Lord God called unto Adam, and said into him, Where art thou? [10] And he said, I heard thy voice in the garden, and I was afraid, because I was naked; and I hid myself.[11] And he said, Who told thee that thou wast naked? Hast, thou eaten of the tree, whereof I commanded thee that thou shouldest not eat?" The devil is always bringing sins into your life because he knows that the more, you sin the more you lose your spiritual authority and you just become ordinary. Without spiritual authority, you cannot have dominion and you cannot enjoy the life of the kingdom of God here on earth now.

18

Belief

Mark 9: 23 -24 [23] "Jesus said unto him, If thou canst believe, all things are possible to him that believeth. [24] And straightway the father of the child cried out, and said with tears, Lord, I believe; help thou mine unbelief." There is natural belief and spiritual belief. We use natural belief in the physical things of this world and spiritual belief in the life of the kingdom of God. Spiritual belief deals with the unseen world, it sees the unseen and believes in the unseen. Natural belief works with the flesh, spiritual belief works with the spirit man. Spiritual belief is brought by the word of God and the spirit of God. Spiritual belief causes you to live a supernatural life. Natural belief has got nothing to do with God it believes in the seen world. Natural belief says if I cannot see it with my physical eyes then that thing does not exist and cannot be true.

Spiritual belief comes from the word of God and the spirit of God. Spiritual belief produces or gives birth to faith. You cannot have faith in God without first believing in him. Matthew 17:20 "And Jesus said unto them, because of your unbelief: for verily I say unto you, If ye have faith as a grain of mustard seed, ye shall say unto this mountain, Remove hence to yonder place; and it shall remove. And nothing shall be impossible unto you." Belief either natural or spiritual comes from what you have learnt through doctrine, experience, or seen others doing physically or spiritually. Natural belief does not work in the kingdom of God, unfortunately, many Christians try to use this kind of belief and that is why many are discouraged and do not know what to do next. You get spiritual belief by understanding from scriptures through the Holy Spirit who God is and your dealings and experiences with him on a day-to-day basis. As you study the word of God you understand his ways and then you believe in him.

David had belief in God because he had dealings with him as he was looking after his father's sheep. 1Samuel 17: 34 -37 [34] And David said unto Saul, Thy servant kept his father's sheep, and there came a lion, and a bear, and took a lamb out of the flock; [35] And I went out after him, and smote him, and delivered it out of his mouth: and when he arose against me, I caught him by his beard, and smote him, and slew him.[36] Thy servant slew both the lion and the bear; and this circumcised Philistine shall be as one of them, seeing he hath defied the armies of the living God. [37] David said moreover, The Lord that delivered me out of the paw of the lion, and out of the paw of a bear, he will deliver me out of the hand of this Philistine. And Saul said unto David, Go, and the Lord be with thee." When you believe in something you start to live what you believe, or you live your belief and that is faith. When you believe in God you start to live his word doing what it says and that is faith. You cannot act upon what you do not believe in. I sit on a chair because I believe that it has the capacity to carry me. My action of sitting on the chair is my faith based on the information that the chair can carry me.

Many Christians talk about their faith in God, but they do not have enough of the word that can bring belief to them. We get all the promises of God to work in our lives when we believe. You cannot believe in something that you do not know. Knowledge of the word of God gives birth to belief and belief gives birth to faith and faith gives birth to the manifestation of what you believed in. Your natural beliefs and past experiences always fight against your spiritual belief and you find it hard to embrace the new things that God wants to do to you. God wants to do new things in your life, he can only do the new things through his word and his spirit. Isaiah 43:18-19 [18] "Remember ye not the former things, neither consider the things of old.[19] Behold, I will do a new thing; now it shall spring forth; shall ye not know it? I will even make a way in the wilderness, and rivers in the desert." The new thing that God wants to do in your life is through the spiritual belief not through the natural belief. When you believe the word of God all things are possible therefore you are limiting yourself you cannot blame anyone even God himself, JUST BELIEVE and all is yours.

19

The Character of God

Having the character of God does not come automatically when you get born again. You must work out your own character by the word of God after being born again. Working out your character is not a day's job it is a lifetime job. You must always strive to live a better life and have the character of Christ until you die. Without the word of God, it is impossible to have the character of Jesus Christ. You learn about him from the word of God through the power of the Holy Spirit. First, we must work to have the mindset of Christ without the mindset of Christ you cannot have the character of God. We learn the mindset of Jesus Christ from the word of God therefore the word is central in having the character of God. The mindset regulates and controls how you think, what you think is what you do, and what you do creates habits and those habits are your character.

What is character? It is the group of qualities and traits that make you a person. The traits for example are generosity, integrity, loyalty, devotion, loving, sincerity, self-control, etc. Character is developed either positively or negatively through our experiences and things that we choose to learn and do. Therefore, to have the character of God you must have experiences with him and learn his ways from his word.

People get attacked by demons because of their characters, the way you live attracts either God or demons. If you live righteously God is attracted to you, if you live unrighteously demons are attracted to your life and they get into you and start to control your life. Character is the doorway of spiritual forces good or bad into your life.

Character brings curses or blessings into someone's life. The blessings of God do not come into our life through prayer they come through your character. The character of God attracts the blessings of God in your life, therefore develop your character every day by studying the word of God and practicing it. Knowing the word of God only without living it cannot give you the character of God. The more you have the character of God the more effective you become in the kingdom of God and a threat you become in the kingdom of darkness.

Many people are suffering in their lives because of their characters, they are not aware that they are able to change their characters, some say that they are born the way that they are, they cannot change. Nobody is born with a certain character, you are born with no character you start to develop it as a child by seeing what the people around you are doing and you start to do the same, but when you grow up you have the power to change if you want and you can change.

Saul lost his kingship because of his character 1 Samuel 13: 14 "But now thy kingdom shall not continue: the Lord hath sought him a man after his own heart, and the Lord hath commanded him to be captain over his people, because thou hast not kept that which the Lord commanded thee," Marriages are being destroyed because of bad characters, jobs are being lost as well even opportunities, etc. If all the people in the world had the character of God, there would no wars no problems at all but the opposite is true. When you study the word of God it helps you to discover weaknesses in your character. You must not rely on what you think about yourself. All people think that they are good they only do bad things because of other people.

Do not trust your heart trust the word of God. Jeremiah 17:9 "The heart is deceitful above all things, and desperately wicked who can know it." Work on your character every day through the word of God. The character of God gives you spiritual authority which you need to dominate and subdue the world a mandate that you were given by God. You are born in the kingdom of God as a child of God, but you must on daily basis develop to be like Christ, live, think and do things like Christ through the word of God. You must develop your character so that you may become a servant of God and even a friend of God. You do not become a servant of God by just being born again but by developing the character of God.

Develop your character to become a servant of the Lord, servants of the Lord are men of character, they have the character of God. Being a servant of God demands the manifestation of God through your life. People see God in your day-to-day living not only when you are in church. Many think that everyone who preaches the word of God or who goes to church is a servant of God but it is far from it. Servants of God are seen by their characters, when you get closer to them you smell and see Christ in them, they are above reproach.

They continue in the word of God John 8:31 "Then Jesus said to those Jews which believed on him, If you continue in my word, then are ye my disciples indeed;" When you have the character of God, God will always reveal his secrets to you. Amos 3:7 "Surely the Lord God will do nothing, but he revealeth his secret unto his servants the prophets." The character of God does not come by just being drunk of the Holy Spirit, speaking in other tongues and laughing in the spirit. You must be sober and allow the Holy Spirit to show you through the word of God where you need to change and you start to work to change, also accept correction from other people they know you better than yourself you are biased to yourself. The people that you spend more time with shape your character as well as the environment. Proverbs 13:20 "He that walketh with wise men shall be wise: but a companion of fools shall be destroyed." You must spend more time with God for you to be like him. Psalm 1:1 "Blessed is the man that walketh not in the counsel of the ungodly, nor standeth in the way of sinners, nor sitteth in the seat of the scornful."

To have the character of God the word of God must be the standard of your life.

You cannot have the character of God if you are only interested in the verses in the word of God that do not rebuke and correct you. Real change comes when we get rebuked and corrected. 2 Timothy 3:16 "All scripture is God -breathed and is useful for instruction, for conviction, for correction, and for training in righteousness," What makes us children of God and for us to inherit the kingdom of God is Jesus manifested in us through the character of God and not spiritual gifts that we may have. The word of God does not change you it points to you where you must change. After the word has shown you then you must decide to change.

When the word of God shows you must be angery with those issues and have a desire to change. Start to control yourself and deal with the issues. If you suffer from anger you must learn how to deal with your anger until you are no more an angry person. If you discover that your anger is demonic you must cast out the demon in the name of Jesus Christ. You must fight to have a godly character it does not come easily. If you inherited your character traits from your forefathers, you still must fight with those things with the help of the Holy Spirit until you over- come. You can have the character of God by engaging yourselves in the school of God. The teacher in the school of God is the

Holy Spirit who teaches you the word of God and the ways of God. Jesus Christ must become my best companion for me to develop the character of God.

20

God cannot take you to your destiny without your involvement.

Change in your life is not an event but it is a process, and that process involves you and God. The church or the leader of your church cannot bring change directly to your life. The work of the church is to connect you to Jesus Christ. After the connection, you must stay connected and develop your relationship with God by the word of God. God takes you to your destiny by his word, he instructs you step by step as he takes you there. As you cooperate with him by doing what he instructs you that is how you advance to your destiny day by day. John 10:27 "My sheep hear my voice, and I know them, and they follow me:" The relationship that you develop with God determines the magnitude of the change that you are going to have. The relationship is developed by the word of God ignoring it is ignoring your destiny. Many Christians are connected to their churches but not to God and they do not have any time to study the word of God. They do not know the importance of the word of God. They think that change comes if God wants to change them if he does not it is all up to him. They are not aware that God wants to change everybody, and not some people. Jesus Christ died on the cross to change all the people not some.

The purpose of the church is there to teach you the word of God but you must put it into practice. Change in your life is determined by the way you live or practice the word of God. In secular school, the school does not make you what you become in life, but they give you knowledge that you must use to become what you want to be. Some people think that change in their lives comes by being prayed for by their Pastor, but it does not work that way. The Pastor is there to assist but he is limited. You must get involved yourself by the word of God. God is the one who knows your destiny and he is calling you by his word and taking you to that destiny. Jeremiah 29:11 "For I know the thoughts that I think toward you, saith the Lord, thoughts of peace, and not of evil, to give you an expected end." God had the destiny for Abraham, but that plan was never going to work if Abraham did not cooperate with God. He obeyed the instructions of God and did what God instructed him to do. If he had refused to do what God instructed, he was never going to be what we know him today.

God did not superimpose himself upon Abraham he respected his choice and asked him, and he responded positively. This is how God takes you to your destiny. Genesis 12:1 -4 [1] Now the Lord had said unto Abram, get thee out of thy country, and from thy kindred, and from thy father's house, unto a land that I will shew thee:[2] And I will make of thee a great nation, and I will bless thee, and make thy name great; and thou shalt be a blessing:[3] And I will bless them that bless thee, and curse him that curseth thee: and in thee shall all families of the earth be blessed. [4] So Abram departed, as the Lord had spoken unto him; and Lot went with him: and Abram was seventy and five years old when he departed out of Haran."

Hearing from God on a day-to-day basis is very important because without hearing from him you lose focus. If Abraham did not hear God and what God told him to do he could have lost everything and could not have reached to his destiny. The devil is very much aware that change in our lives comes by the word of God which is why he fights not to allow you to study the word seriously. He is delighted when you become a religious person. Religion has nothing to do with the word of God it is all about useless rituals and church traditions. Change and success for your life rest upon you and God working together through his word.

Today there is so much prominence of the so-called prophets who claim that they have the ability from God to change people and many are running to them but very little is happening. They sell some oil or water which they say has the power of God to change people. God does not need oil or water to help his word to accomplish what he sends the word to go and do. The word of God is enough to bring change to your life. That oil and water they are using is not from God, but it is from the world of darkness. The powers at work in that oil or water are satanic powers, marine spirits are involved in those heal- ings, etc. Those leaders who use water to do miracles get their powers from marine spirits. People can get healed and see miracles through those things, but it is not God performing those miracles. Real change comes from God, it involves you and God, his word, and the power of the Holy Spirit period.

Change that comes from God is traceable but change from the world of darkness is not. God had a plan to transform the widow of Zarephath he went to her and spoke to her through the prophet. For the woman to be transformed she had to cooperate with God first. If she rebelled, she was going to remain poor and even die of hunger. God had a plan to deliver her from the famine, but it was all centered on her reaction to what God said. God has the best plan for you but for him to go ahead with the plan you must accept what he asks you to do through his word if you refuse you will continue in that situation no change.

Many people blame God for lives that are not changing, it is not the problem of God. The problem is you who is not hearing what God is saying to you. You must hear what he is saying, if you follow what he is saying, and you do what he asks you to do change will definitely come. Change is your positive response to the word of God. God has never hidden anything from man it is all in his word it is all up to you how you deal with his word. When God sent the angel of death in Egypt he told the children of Israel what they were supposed to do in order for them not to get killed, if they did not do what he had instructed they were all going to be killed even if they were his people. Therefore, it is very important to listen and to do what God instructs.

He does not work with you and me without giving instructions. What you do with his word is the result you will get. God does not change you because you are special, he changes us all if we do what he instructs us to do by his word. Obedience is key to every change that comes from God. Refusing to follow what he says takes you to your destruction and total failure. Isaiah 1:19 "If ye be willing and obedient, ye shall eat the good of the land."

21

Principles

God does not work anyhow but he works upon principles. He has put principles that control this physical world for example the principle of gravity etc. There are also principles that run the kingdom of God in which you find yourself in when you get born again. You must spend much time studying the principles so that you understand how to do things and operate in that new kingdom. The kingdom of God is totally different from the other world that you were born in biologically. All the principles of the kingdom of God are in his word. If you are ignorant of the word of God, there is no way that you may understand the principles. Hosea 4: 6 "My people are destroyed for lack of knowledge: because thou hast rejected knowledge, I will also reject thee, that thou shalt be no priest to me: seeing thou hast forgotten the law of thy God, I will also forget thy children." The principles do not change it is you who must change, some try to change them to suit what they want.

Principles are fundamental rules that cannot be changed about how something is done or made. If you do not know these principles, you will always be frustrated and you always do not get what you are supposed to get because you will be doing things the wrong way. Zeal only without knowledge of his word has discouraged so many. You must know for example the principles of prayer, do not just pray the way you think you ought to pray there are principles that you must follow. Romans 10:1 -3 [1] Brethren, my heart's desire and prayer to God for Israel is , that they might be saved. [2] For I bear them record that they have a zeal of God, but not according to knowledge. [3] For they being ignorant of God's righteousness, and going about to establish their own righteousness, have not submitted themselves unto the righteousness of God."

God is the same yesterday today and forever and his principles do not change as well forever. Hebrews 13:8 "Jesus Christ the same yesterday, and today, and forever." Heaven and earth shall pass away but his word and his ways abide forever. Many Christians have a rough idea of how they are supposed to do things in the kingdom of God, but they do not have full knowledge therefore they do things halfway and they think that is all they need to do and because of that they do not get the results that they expect. When you do not get the expected results check why and correct where you need to correct, God is never wrong it is only you who can be wrong.

Hebrews 11:6 says, "But without faith it is impossible to please him: for he that cometh to God must believe that he is, and that he is a rewarder of them that diligently seek him." This is another principle in the kingdom of God, nothing works in the king- dom of God without faith. You must understand what governs faith you must be sure if you have true faith or not because this is the only thing that pleases God. Without the word of God, you cannot develop faith. I have heard many people say they have faith and yet they do not spend time studying the word of God, what they have is natural faith that everybody else has in the world not real faith. With spiritual faith all things are possible, and nothing can stop you if you have it.

I have discovered that because many Christians do not spend much time in the word of God, they are living basing their Christianity on hearsay information. They can quote certain verses from the bible, but they have never seen those verses in the bible themselves. To make progress in your life understand the principles of God by his word and study and understand his word progressively, live it progressively, believe it progressively, live in the spirit progressively, prophesy it upon your life progressively, meditate upon it progressively, and have hope in God progressively and be open to learning progressively.

Do not measure your speed of change or progress with other people you just continue doing what you are supposed to do with the word of God and God is always faithful for your time will come. Learn thoroughly from the word of God through the help of the Holy Spirit how certain things must be done. It is very easy to assume that you can do certain things the way you think they should be done. Do not believe things that you hear other people saying pertaining to the things of God, verify everything by the word of God yourself. Even if your leader says something is not a sin, verify it by the word of God because he might be wrong. Everything in the world is done according to a certain formula but when it comes to the things of God people think they can be done anyhow no. Everything in the kingdom of God has got a way it must be done if you are to get the results that God says you will get.

If the word of God says you must believe in God, it follows that if you do not believe you will get nothing from him. It is something that you must make sure you develop before you go far, you cannot ignore this and think things will work for you. Principles are foundational pillars that you must make sure you have developed before you continue moving on in the kingdom of God. There is no excuse for doing things wrongly and thinking that God will understand that you did not know.

He does not accept that because he has written everything down for you to study and has also given you the Holy Spirit to interpret the scriptures to give you a better understanding, therefore ignorance is no defense. People want to give excuses of the devil for not doing the right things, Jesus dealt with the devil on the cross and he finished him, he has no power over you at all. He cannot stop you; you are living far above him. There is no valid excuse for you not to know how you must operate in the kingdom of God.

22

Revelation from the word of God brings a revolution in your life

As you study the word of God you must have revelation from that word otherwise the word only without revelation cannot bring change in your life. Revelation according to google is" Uncovering and bringing to light of that which had been previously wholly hidden or only obscurely seen." Revelation is a surprising divine disclosure of mysteries hidden in the word of God. There are mysteries hidden in the word of God that you will only understand by revelation. Revelation completes your understanding of the word of God, without it you have not yet understood the word that you have read.

Revelation is a very important aspect when dealing with the word of God. The word of God is spiritual, and it must be understood spiritually, you cannot say you are understanding it without revelation. Revelation is seeing and understanding the spiritual things of God or of the kingdom of God. It is a dramatic disclosure of something not previously known pertaining to the kingdom of God. Revelation is the supernatural communication of the truth of God to your spirit by the Holy Spirit. God transforms your life through revelation, when he speaks to you, and you do not get a revelation of what he is saying it means you have not heard him.

Without revelation you cannot know God, God must show himself in your spirit for you to know him. There are many who go to church and do everything that is done in church, but God has never shown or revealed himself to those individuals. You get connected with God by revelation, you see God with your spiritual eyes, and it is as real as meeting God in person. When God reveals himself to you spiritually your experience with Jesus is not different from that of the disciples who met him physically. The disciples were not better exposed to Jesus than you and me who are meeting with him spiritually. If there is a difference, then God is unfair to us. This is why Paul was even more effective than even those who ate and lived with Jesus physically.

When you have revelation from the word of God you cannot stop reading it, it is exciting and fascinating. To have a revelation you must create an atmosphere for it by being prayerful, being holy, studying and meditating upon the word of God, must have hunger and thirst for God and living in the spirit, and make sure you are filled by the Holy Spirit. 1 Corinthians 2:10 -11 [10] But God hath revealed them unto us by his Spirit: for the Spirit searcheth all things, yea, the deep things of God. [11] For what man knoweth the things of a man, save the spirit of man which is in him? Even so, the things of God knoweth no man, but the spirit of God."

God reveals his word to us to change us. Revelation makes you understand spiritually what God is saying to you and what action you must do. Revelation gives you an inner push that you find very hard to resist to want to do what God is asking you to do. It gives you the urgency to do what God is instructing you to do through his word. Without revelation that push is not there, and the urgency is not there, usually you will not do what the word is instructing you to do you are full of doubt. Revelation takes away doubt from you and you are fast to act upon what God is saying.

When you listen to that push and go-ahead to do the thing that is how your life is revolutionized. Abraham by listening to the urgency and the push acted in obedience to God and his life was totally changed and he became another man that is why everything about him changed.

David received a revelation from God that is why he was ready to fight Goliath and that totally changed his life from a shepherd boy to a king. Paul on his way to Damascus got a revelation and the revelation turned his life around from a murderer to an apostle of God. Revelation from God changes everything about you, it takes you to higher levels of your life, it gives you a new perspective, you start to see new horizons and it gives you a new vision. Paul received a new vision instead of destroying the saints he became a preacher of the gospel that he was fighting against all his life. Abraham was an idol worshipper with his father when he got the revelation, he was made the father of all nations, the friend of God, and was made to bless all the families of the earth. I have seen the revelation of God taking me from being a useless somebody to who I am today. I do not have time to get into all that revelation has done to my life in this book, but you will get that in my other book when I write where God picked me up from, but for now just know that the revelation of God through his word has revolutionized my life to where I am today and the same revelation can do the same to your life.

Revelation gives you the ability to see in your spirit what the word of God is speaking about, it is dramatically made alive in your spirit. Abraham saw the land in his spirit that God was talking about where he was taking him. When you get a revelation from God other people do not see what you see. Therefore, do not listen to them when they are stopping you it is about you and God not them go ahead and do what God is saying to you. Many people want the approval of other people if you do that you lose what God is preparing for you. Abraham listened to God if he had listened to his siblings, he would never have gone to do what God was showing him and he was going to lose everything. Same with David if he listened to his brothers, he was never going to be king.

When God wants to transform your life, he deals with youas an individual do not wait for others to join you or to approve what you are doing. When you have a revelation, the devil will always raise people to stop you. Do not stop go ahead you will enjoy it in the end. Change comes to you when you see it in your spirit first through reve- lation and there is no revelation without the word of God. Revelation gives you vision of your life. Proverbs 29:18 "Where there is no vision, the people perish: but he that keepeth the law, happy is he." Joseph got a vision of his life through revelation which is why he did not handle himself anyhow. When you have a vision, you are not careless with your life. That is why Joseph did not sleep with Potiphar's wife, vision gives you discipline, understanding, and wisdom.

Every revelation comes to transfer you from one point to another in your life if follow the instructions of God. People are missing things because they are not in the right position to get revelations. Stay in the word of God to get revelations from God. You cannot get revelation if you are always busy with the world and if you live in sin you cannot have revelation Proverbs 28:13 "He that covereth his sins shall not prosper: but whoso confesseth and foresaketh them shall have mercy." Do not despise revelation, it is more powerful than education, I am not saying do not go to school, school is good but pursue after revelation as well you will be surprised where it will take you to.

Revelation can catapult a poor man from nothing and get sitted with kings. 1 Samuel 2:8 "He raises up the poor out of the dust, and lifteth up the beggar from the dunghill, to set them among princes, and to make them in- herit the throne of glory: for the pillars of the earth are the Lord's, and he hath set the world upon them." Do not miss a revelation missing it delays you from getting where God is taking you to. Position your- self to capture every opportunity that God gives you. Your change and next move in your life are attached to a revelation. Changes to another level of your business, family, and career are attached to a revelation. Always live in the spirit so that when God brings a revelation you are able to understand it. Revelation is spiritual therefore you capture it spiritually your natural mind cannot process it it's beyond the scope of your human mind.

23

Good heart?

Matthew 5:8 "Blessed are the pure in heart :for they shall see God."

The word of God clearly gives us the condition of the heart of every man but for us to see God we must have a pure heart . It means just being born again is not the only thing that you need to have for you to see God. What it means then is that after being born again you must work to have a pure heart, my salvation does not give me an automatic pure heart. I need the word of God to take out what is originally full in my heart to have a pure heart. What is in my heart that I need to take out of it? Mark 7:21-23 [21] "For from within, out of the heart of men, proceed evil thoughts, adulteries, fornications, murders,[22] Thefts, covetousness, wickedness, deceit, lasciviousness, an evil eye, blasphemy, pride, foolishness:[23] All these evil things come from within, and defile the man." Jeremiah 17: 9-10 [9] "The heart is deceitful above all things, and desperately wicked: who can know it?[10] I the Lord search the heart. I try the reins, even to give every man according to his ways, and according to the fruit of his doings." What you have read from the scriptures above are the things that are in every man's heart. The condition of your heart is desperately bad, but you need a pure heart to see God.

If then you continue with this heart it means that you cannot see God. It all demands the cleansing of that heart by the word of God. Many Christians are not working upon their hearts they think that once they are born again and go to a certain church and follow the programs there that is all that they need to see God. The heart of a man is very bad even without demons. Many times, people always say it is the devil who causes them to do certain things. That is not always true I have learnt that man is capable of doing any- thing without demons influencing him because of his heart.

Now before we continue with this topic let us stop for a moment and see what we call the heart, what is it. A human being is made up of three components, body, soul, and spirit these three are intrinsically connected, the connection is highly complicated we need the grace of God to understand how they work together. This is what google says about the heart. "The heart is the locus of physical and spiritual being and represents the central wisdom of feeling as opposed to the head-wisdom of reason. It is compassion and understanding, life-giving and complex. It is a symbol of love. Often known as the seat of emotions, the heart is synonymous with affection. Basically, the soul is the person/ life force, and the heart is the inner seat of motivation. Research shows that the heart does not just take commands from the brain - heart – brain communication is a dynamic, two-way conversation. Most of your decisions are made at the heart level, and then you justify them with your logical thinking head brain."

The heart is connected to the brain they work together, the heart is your emotions and with your brain, they constitute the soul of a man. Your heart and your brain are not born again when you get born again, what gets born again is your spirit part. You need the word of God to be able to control your soul. Without the word of God, you are at the mercy of your soul. If you do not have the word of God, your soul takes control of everything that you do according to what is full in the heart. Ezekiel 36:26-27 [26] A new heart also will I give you, and a new spirit will put within you : and I will give you an heart of flesh. [27] And I will put my spirit within you, and cause you to walk in my statutes, and ye shall keep my judge- ments, and do them." Reading these verses, I used to think that when one gets born again and filled by the Holy Spirit, he automatically gets a good heart. But I now know that it does not work that way. It is not an automatic thing I have to study the word of God spiritually as I do that by feeding my spirit man, he becomes stronger and gets the ability to control the soul.

You are not going to be able to remove those bad things that are in your heart you can only suppress them by the word of God through your spirit. What is in your heart is only going to be dealt with finally when your soul gets redeemed by Jesus Christ when he comes to take the saints when you shall be like him.1 Corinthians 15:51-53 [51] "Behold, I shew you a mystery; We shall not all sleep, but we shall all be changed, [52] In a moment, in the twinkling of an eye, at the last trumpet shall sound, and the dead shall be raised changed.{53] For this corruptible must put on incorruption, and this mortal must put on immortality." The biggest work that you have now is to fight the soul with the word of God. Romans 7:21 "I find then a law, that, when I would do good, evil is present with me. [22] For I delight in the law of God after the inward man: [23] "But I see another law in my members, warring against the law of my mind, and bringing me into captivity to the law of sin which is in my members. "

Many times, Christians think that they have good hearts, but I say just wait until one day you go through some challenging situations, or someone does something wrong to you that is when you will discover how wicked or bad you are. You cannot have a good heart by just praying to God to give you a good heart, as you pray you must practice living the word of God that will give you a good heart. All human beings got a bad heart when Adam and Eve disobeyed God and by doing that, they automatically inherited all that was in the devil and those things are found in every man's heart. We continue to develop this bad heart by the things that we went through as we were growing up, the environments that we grew up in, the bad things that we inherited from our forefathers, the bad things that we saw others doing and we started doing them as well. There is no way that we may have good hearts if we do not stay in the word of God and allow it to work in us. Psalm 119:11 "Thy word have I hid in mine heart, that I might not sin against thee." Romans 12:2 "And be not conformed to this world: but be ye transformed by the renewing of your mind, that ye may prove what is that good, and acceptable, and perfect, will of God."

The deceitful heart that you continue to have is the biggest problem that is blocking you from seeing the hand of God and to live the Life of the Kingdom of God. Isaiah 59: 2-4 [2] But your iniquities have separated between you and God, and your sins have hid his face from you, that he will not hear.[3] For your hands are defiled with blood, and your fingers with iniquity; your lips have spoken lies, your tongue hath muttered perverseness. [4] None calleth for justice, nor any pleadeth for truth: they trust in vanity, and speak lies; they conceive mischief, and bring forth iniquity." The heart is the source of all sins not demons as I used to think, demons will get involved but everything is initiated from the heart.

You are failing to dominate and subdue the world because of the sins that are in your heart, you are being led by these things instead of the word of God and your spirit. You were mandated by God to dominate the world. Genesis 1:28 "And God blessed them, and God said unto them, Be fruitful, and multiply, and replenish the earth, and subdue it:

and have dominion over the fish of the sea, and over the fowl of the air, and over every living thing that moveth upon the earth."

Demons operate in your life because they are attracted by the bad things that are in your heart already. Demons could not enter the life of Jesus Christ because he had a pure heart. John 14:30 "Hereafter I will not talk much with you: for the prince of the world cometh, and hath nothing in me." The devil comes into you because you have his things in your heart. As a child of God, you must not be led by your heart but be led by your spirit man and the word of God. You are three in one body, soul, and spirit as we have seen already.

The heart is the soul therefore you must be led by the spirit man. In essence a human being is spirit and should be led by the spirit of God by the word of God. Galatians 5:16-17 [16] This I say then, walk in the spirit, and ye shall not fulfil the lust of the flesh. [17] For the flesh lusteth against the Spirit, and the Spirt against the flesh: and these are contrary the one to the other: so that ye cannot do the things that ye would." The more you become spiritual the more you can control the heart, the soul. You become more spiritual by having more of the word of God, by feeding the spirit man with the word of God. You will continue to have wicked thoughts here and there etc but having those thoughts is not sin it becomes sin when you continue to entertain them and meditate upon them and do what the thoughts demand done.

When you are spiritual, you can quickly kick off these thoughts out as they are sent from the heart. Psalm 119:11 "Thy word have I hid in mine heart, that I might not sin against thee." Without the word of God, you are going to be led by your heart whether you like it or not. The more you have the word of God and the Holy Spirit at work in your life the more you can live above the desires of your heart, you live a spiritual life. You can only get a good heart from the spirit man when he is full of the word of God.

Jesus lives in the heart of your spirit that is the only way you can have a good heart as you operate spiritually. Galatians 5:22-25 [22] But the fruit of the Spirit is love, joy, peace, longsuffering, gentleness, faith, [23] Meekness, temperance: against such there is no law. [24] And they that are Christ's have cruci- fied the flesh with the affections and lusts. [25] If we live in the Spirit, let us also walk in the Spirit."

You can never be a good person if you are operating from the heart or soul because the heart of every man is full of wickedness until he dies. The wicked things that are in your heart soul you can never take them out to have a good heart, they will only be taken away by Christ when he comes for the second time. You can only have a pure heart by operating from your spirit man he is the one with a pure heart because of the word of God that you feed him with and that is where Christ lives. This is the biggest problem that we have many Christians do not know how to operate spiritually. Spirituality is brought by the word of God which is spirit, the Holy Spirit, and your spirit. When these work together and connect you become a spiritual person. You can operate spiritually without the involvement of your soul and body ,this is how Christ was operating. This demands some work, but it is achievable if it was not achievable God was never going to ask us to live spiritually. Galatians 5:25 "If we live in the spirit, let us also walk in the spirit." What this verse is telling is that let us not be led by our hearts the soul but we must be led by our spirit man who has a good pure heart.

24

Leadership In the Kingdom of God

In this chapter I am going to be talking about leadership you may not be a leader now but one day you are going to be one. You also need to know what is expected from those who lead you so that you may not be led by the wrong people. A leader cannot lead the people of God if he does not live the word of God that he teaches. Leadership in the kingdom of God is all about ushering change and development into the lives of the people that are being led. Without the leader being changed by the word of God he cannot change others by the same word. The word must first transform him both spiritually and physically. Jesus Christ is the word, he did not live another life that was different from what he was teaching, his teaching and his life were one. People can only be changed by the life of the leader and not by what he says only. When a leader says some things, people will not do those things quickly, naturally, they watch and see if the leader is doing it and then they will do it. Leadership in the kingdom of God is not about knowing how to lead, theories of leadership only do not work, people need to copy a life. Jesus came to give life and the leader must give that same life to others.

Character and discipline which are key in leadership can only come into the leader's life when he lives the word of God. 1 Samuel 12:2-4 [2] "And now, behold, the king walketh before you: and I am old and gray-headed; and, behold, my sons are with you: and I have walked before you from my childhood unto this day. [3] Behold, here I am: witness against me before the Lord, and before his anointed: whose ox have I taken? Or whose ass have I taken? Or whom have I defrauded? Whom have I oppressed? Or of whose hand have I received any bribe to blind mine eyes therewith? And I will restore it to you. [4] And they said, Thou hast not defrauded us, nor oppressed us, neither hast thou taken ought of any man's hand." The integrity of a leader and the fear of God comes from the word of God and it gives a leader the character of God.

A leader can teach what he knows but he produces who he is. People come to church because they are tired of their lives, they want new things. The life of the leader must attract people to want to come to Christ who is the answer to their problems. 1 Timothy 4:12 "Let no man despise thy youth; but be thou an example of the believers, in word, in conversation, in charity, in spirit, in faith, in purity." The word of God is asking the leader to be an example in everything to the people that he leads. People are spirits they tap from the spiritual life of their leader. If the leader is not genuine by and by, they will know it, this is the problem of leading spiritual people. A leader must continue to fellowship with God through his word and the Holy Spirit if he does not he will become dry, empty and people will not get anything that is spiritually profitable to them.

The leader is there to help people get connected with their God through his word. Moses brought the children of Israel because of what

God was saying to him in the mountain. Without fellowship with God, the leader has nothing to give to the people. People are not changed physically by God directly; God starts to change them spiritually and then the change will affect them physically.

If there is no training of the people through the word of God, they cannot tap the spiritual changes that God is doing in their lives. There is no change that God does that is outside his word. Therefore, the word of God should be taught to the people otherwise there is no change that is going to come to them. If God is not changing the leader through his word, that leader cannot in turn influence others with his life. John 13:14 -15 [14] "If I then, your Lord and Master, have washed your feet; ye also ought to wash one another's feet. [15] For I have given you an example, that ye should do as I have done to you." Leadership in the kingdom of God is about giving what the leader has received from God. He receives the things of God by his word, without it the leader has nothing to give to the people who are coming after him. Acts 3:6 "Then Peter said, Silver and gold have I none; but such as I have give I thee: In the name of Jesus Christ of Nazareth rise up and walk." Matthew 10:8 "Heal the sick, cleanse the lepers, raise the dead, cast out devils ye have received, freely give."

The leader gets filled by the word of God and when he is full he is able to give it to others Matthew 5:6 "Blessed are they which do hunger and thirst after righteousness: for they shall be filled." The leader must always be full of God because people come to drink from him. A leader in the kingdom of God must have the ability to teach the word of God effectively because it is through the word of God that God is going to change lives. The word of God is the weapon of change, success, and prosperity. Joshua 1:8 "This book of the law shall not depart out of thy mouth; but thou shalt meditate therein day and night, that thou mayest observe to do according to all that is written therein: for then thou shalt make thy way prosperous, and then thou shalt have good success."

Hosea 4:6 "My people are destroyed for lack of knowledge: because thou hast rejected knowledge, I will also reject thee, that thou shalt be no priest to me: seeing thou hast forgotten the law of thy God, I will also forget thy children." People are not going to be changed by church programs that have nothing to do with the word of God, but they are changed by the word of God. The Holy Spirit cannot change someone who does not have the word of God in him.

A leader is a man of Faith but without the word, there is no faith. Romans 10:17 "So then faith cometh by hearing, and hearing by the word of God." In the word of God Caleb encouraged the people when they were discouraged because he had faith in God. People come to the leader discouraged and devastated, they need someone who can revive and encourage them. This cannot happen if the leader is empty without the word of God. Numbers 13:30 "And Caleb stilled the people before Moses and said, Let us go up at once, and possess it; for we are well able to overcome it." People always feel that they are not capable they need someone to encourage them from the word of God. When people are encouraged by the word of God even the weak become strong, and those who are afraid become as bold as a lion.

25

Faith

In the kingdom of God, we operate by faith, without it we cannot please God.1 John 5:4-5 [4] "For whatsoever is born of God overcometh the world: and this is the victory that overcometh the world, even our faith.[5] Who is he that overcometh the world, but he that believeth that Jesus is the Son of God?" It is the word of God that gives us the ability to walk by faith because faith comes by believing the word of God. 2 Corinthians 5:7 "For we walk by faith, not by sight." As a child of God, you must live by faith not by what you see with physical eyes. The word of God gives us spiritual eyes to see where God is taking us and children of God must live by faith. Hebrews 10:38 "Now the just shall live by faith: but if any man draw back, my soul shall have no pleasure in him."

Faith is a walk that you must walk every day of your life not something that you can do sometimes. You must live a life of faith-based on believing and doing what God instructs you to do through his word by his Spirit. There is natural faith and spiritual faith. Spiritual faith does not originate from you it is imparted into your life as you study and meditate on the word of God through the Holy Spirit. Romans 10:17 "So then faith cometh by hearing, and hearing by the word of God." Faith is not convincing yourself that something is true, it is believing what God says by his word and acting upon it. James 1: 22-25 [22] "But be ye doers of the word, and not hearers only, deceiving your own selves.[23] For if any be a hearer of the word, and not a doer, he is like unto a man beholding his natural face in a glass:[24] For he beholdeth himself, and goeth his way, and straightway forgotten what manner of a man he was.[25] But whoso looketh into the perfect law of liberty, and continueth therein, he being not a forgetful hearer, but a doer of the work, this man shall be blessed in his deed."

Many Christians are faithful, but they do not have faith. They are faithful to do what their churches and leaders tell them to do but they do not have faith in God. To have faith in God demands the word of God but many have no time for the word of God. You must be faithful and have faith in God. You use faith to fight your situations, demons and the devil.2 Timothy 4:7 -8 [7] "I have fought a good fight, I have finished my course, I have kept the faith:[8] Henceforth there is laid up for me a crown of righteousness, which the Lord, the righteous judge, shall give me at that day: and not to me only, but unto all them also that love his appearing." Ephesians 6:10 "Finally, my brethren, be strong in the Lord, and in the power of his might." We cannot stand strong without faith and faith comes from the word of God. Faith does not work with your natural mind it works with your spiritual mind. Faith is our positive response to divine revelation.

Abraham received divine revelation through the word of God. He stepped out in obedience to the instructions of God. He did not follow what he wanted but he followed what God instructed him to do and this is faith. Genesis 12 :1 -4 [1] "Now the Lord had said unto Abram, get thee out of thy country, and from thy kindred, and from thy father's house, unto a land that I will shew thee: [2] And I will make of thee a great nation, and I will bless thee, and make thy name great; and thou shalt be a blessing: [3] And I will bless them that bless thee, and curse him that curseth thee: and in thee shall all families of the earth be blessed. [4] So Abram departed, as the Lord had spoken unto him; and Lot went with him: and Abram was seventy and five years old when he departed out of Haran."

A person gets little faith because he has little of the word of God. Matthew 8:26 "And he saith unto them, why are you fearful, O ye of little faith? Then he arose and rebuked the winds and the sea, and there was a great calm." People with little faith or without faith are full of fear. Faith needs more than an intellectual knowledge of the word of God. You may know it but still do not have faith, as I said earlier you need to understand the word of God spiritually not just intellectually. John 5:39-40 [39] "Search the scriptures; for in them ye think ye have eternal life: and they are they which testify of me. [40] And ye will not come to me, that ye might have life." Faith is the driving force that drives everything in the kingdom of God. It all starts with faith, to be saved you must first believe in Jesus Christ without faith nothing works.

26

Wealth

If you desire to be wealthy, it works with obedience, or I can say obedience attracts wealth from God. Remember all things were created by God and it all belongs to him, therefore, to enjoy what God has, have a strong relationship with him first. The most important thing in that relationship is obedience. Abraham become a wealthy man because he obeyed God and had a very strong relationship with him. He was instructed to leave his country, relatives, and his father's house and go to where God wanted him to go, he went he did not refuse. This was a very big test to leave all those things that he was deeply connected to from birth. As if this was not enough after waiting for many years without a son and he got a son God again asked him to sacrifice the same son to him, he did not refuse but agreed to sacrifice the son. Obedience to the word of God is fundamental in you getting wealthy.

We can go on and on with examples from the word of God for people who became wealthy because of their relationship with God. Another example is Job of Uz. The word of God says that this man was perfect and upright and that he feared God. Job 1:1 "There was a man in the land of Uz, whose name was Job; and that man was perfect and upright, and one that feared God, and eschewed evil." Job became a wealthy man because of his relationship with God who is the source of wealth. The man lived for God and that made him to be wealthy. If you live for yourself only there is no way you can be wealthy, you restrict yourself that way. I have discovered that if I take the vision of God to be my vision and live to fulfill it God will make me wealthy so that I am able to do what God wants to be done on earth. He will give me the financial means to be able to reach many people who have needs to be met. God cannot make you a wealthy man for the sake of making you one and yet you are not serving his purposes.

Vision is important for you to be wealthy let your vision be the same as that of God. Proverbs 29:18 "Where there is no vision, the people perish: but he that keepeth the law, happy is he." You get the vision and purposes of God from his word. When your vision is for the world the salvation of the world God will give you resources for the world but if your vision is just self-centered you just get that which is sufficient for you. The bigger the vision the bigger the provision from God. Every vision starts small, but it does not stay small it continues to grow. As you continue in the word of God that is how the vision grows. Wealth is not for the ignorant and the foolish it is for the wise. The wise are those who know God and live for him. Those who have sold their lives for God. Worldly wisdom is not considered wisdom it is only when you come to the knowledge of Christ that you are considered wise. Wise people have the same vision that God has, that is to save humanity. God loves people if you love his people, and you are concerned about their welfare God will give you what you need to help his people. Many are never going to be wealthy because the reasons why they want those resources are wrong.

27

Conclusion

Jesus Christ has done all that he was meant to do and what he was sent by the Father to come and do here on earth he left nothing undone. He did everything a hundred percent he has put us back to our original position where we had been dethroned by the devil through the disobedience of Adam and Eve. All has been done but that which is not yet done is for you and me to do for us to get results. Through Adam, we failed but through Christ success and prosperity is ours again, but it does not come on a silver platter there is work to be done by you and me. Christ worked so hard that is why he shouted on the cross that it was finished he meant the work that he had come to do was finished. Therefore, if things are not working in your life do not blame God check and find out where you are doing it wrong from his word and do what you are supposed to do in the right manner. You have been empowered and you can do all things through Christ, no demon or devil, man can stop you. You are seated far above every demon or spirit everything is now under your feet but if you are ignorant of the word of God you shall continue to suffer.

Do not worry about what people say about you they despise you because they do not know what God has done in your life. You must not lose focus because of what they say continue to believe what God is saying to you through his word. Do not be just a churchgoer but be a child of God and children of God always hear the voice of the chief shepherd Jesus Christ every day. Hearing from God directly is very important in your life because when you hear from God no man can distract you. There was a time in my life when I used not to study the word of God seriously although I was a Christian one day God opened my spiritual eyes and I decided to study and meditate on it and today I am enjoying every moment of my life because of the revelations that I get each time I study the word. Now I am always hooked up spiritually and continuously live in the spiritual realm even if I am not studying the word, I am continuously in dialogue with the Holy Spirit 24/7. Wow, God is so good and so sweet that is why David one day said, come and taste for he is sweeter than honeycomb indeed he is sweet, but the sweetness cannot be explained with human words. HALLELUJAH!!!!!!!

My brother and sister your church or your Pastor have no capacity to change your life physically and spiritually, God has ordained his word to change your life. Everything about your life is in the word of God. The so-called prophets or any human being in whatever capacity cannot change your life. They claim that they can change your life, but it is a lie if you believe them what they will only end up doing is manipulate your life. They will demand so many things from you even your money in the name of changing your life but later you will realize that your life was better off before you met them. God loves you he has all your solutions in his word which he has given to the world. Pray to get a revelation from God about the importance of the word of God in your life. You are a spirit living in a body and you live by the word of God which is spirit and your Father God is spirit.

Dr Francis Madzivadondo is a seasoned Pastor, ordained in 1990 after three years of training in Biblical Studies and Christian Leadership at Africa Multination For Christ College [AMFCC] in Zimbabwe, a bible college for Forward In Faith Ministries International church.

He holds the following qualifications:

- Diploma in Biblical Studies and Christian Leadership [AMFCC] Zimbabwe Harare.
- Diploma in Community Services – Australia.
- Advanced Diploma in Counselling and Psychology – International Careers Institute – Australia.
- Bachelor's Degree in Christian Education.
- Master's degree In Christian Education
- Doctor of Philosophy in Christian Education – New burgh Theological College -USA.

He is an international Gospel conference and television speaker. He has pastored in many places around Zimbabwe for fourteen years before being sent out to foreign nations as a missionary. He has traveled and worked in other nations as a short-term and long-term missionary. He has worked in Mozambique, South Africa, The Democratic Republic of Congo [DRC], South Pacific Islands of Tonga, Australia, Canada, USA, Belize, United Kingdom. Currently, as the book was being written he was working as a missionary in New Zealand as the National Overseer/National Administrator.

He has written two other books.

1. Pulling Down of Strongholds.
2. Marriage Dynamics.

Dr Francis Madzivadondo is married to Pastor Sandra Madzivadondo and together have five children and five grandchildren to date.

www.ingramcontent.com/pod-product-compliance
Lightning Source LLC
Chambersburg PA
CBHW050317010526
44107CB00055B/2273